THE 15-
MEDITERRANEAN DIET
COOKBOOK

Wholesome and Delicious Mediterranean Dishes in a Flash.
Quick and Flavorful Recipes for Busy Days.

Asher Grant

TABLE OF CONTENTS

INTRODUCTION

Introduction

Welcome to "The 15-Minute Mediterranean Diet Cookbook," a culinary journey that brings the vibrant flavors and healthful benefits of the Mediterranean diet to your kitchen in a time-efficient manner. This cookbook is designed to provide you with a delightful array of easy, flavorful, and nutritious recipes that capture the essence of the Mediterranean lifestyle. Drawing inspiration from the rich culinary traditions of the Mediterranean region, this cookbook offers a diverse selection of dishes that can be prepared in just 15 minutes, making it convenient for modern, busy lifestyles.

Embracing the Mediterranean Diet

"The 15-Minute Mediterranean Diet Cookbook" is a celebration of the renowned Mediterranean diet, known for its emphasis on fresh, whole foods, heart-healthy fats, and an abundance of fruits, vegetables, and lean proteins. This cookbook is a gateway to experiencing the health benefits and culinary pleasures associated with this time-honored way of eating.

Expert Guidance and Nutritious Recipes

Authored by experts in the field of nutrition and Mediterranean cuisine, this cookbook provides a brief introduction to the benefits of the Mediterranean diet, along with practical cooking tips, lifestyle guidance, and a delectable collection of 15-minute recipes. Each recipe is thoughtfully crafted to showcase the simplicity, flavor, and nutritional value of Mediterranean-inspired ingredients, allowing you to savor the essence of the Mediterranean diet in every bite.

A Culinary Adventure Awaits

Whether you are new to the Mediterranean diet or seeking to expand your repertoire of quick and nutritious meals, "The 15-Minute Mediterranean Diet Cookbook" offers a delightful culinary adventure that is both accessible and enriching. From vibrant salads and hearty soups to flavorful main dishes and delectable desserts, this cookbook invites you to embark on a journey of healthful and satisfying eating experiences.

In conclusion, "The 15-Minute Mediterranean Diet Cookbook" is a valuable resource for anyone interested in embracing the Mediterranean diet and savoring its benefits through a delightful collection of quick and easy recipes. Get ready to indulge in the flavors of the Mediterranean and elevate your culinary repertoire with this time-efficient and health-conscious approach to cooking.

The Mediterranean diet is renowned for its numerous health benefits, as supported by various research findings. Here are some key insights from the search results:

1. **Reduced Risk of Chronic Diseases**: The Mediterranean diet has been associated with a reduced risk of developing heart disease, cancer, and type 2 diabetes. By following this diet, individuals may lower their risk of death at any age by 20% and protect against type 2 diabetes, thanks to its rich fiber content that aids in maintaining a healthy weight.
2. **Heart Health**: Studies have linked the Mediterranean diet with lower risk factors for heart disease, such as high cholesterol and high blood pressure. It is recognized as a healthy eating pattern by American nutrition experts and the World Health Organization .
3. **Longevity and Weight Management**: Embracing the Mediterranean diet has been shown to increase longevity and may help prevent weight gain. Additionally, it has been associated with a reduced risk of cognitive decline and may contribute to healthy aging.
4. **Overall Health Benefits**: The Mediterranean diet has been named the top diet by U.S. News & World Report for several consecutive years. It is praised for its potential health benefits, including its preventive effect toward cardiovascular diseases, decreased risk of diabetes and metabolic-related conditions, and potential role in preventing certain cancers .

In conclusion, the Mediterranean diet offers a wide range of health benefits, including reduced risk of chronic diseases, improved heart health, longevity, weight management, and overall well-being. Its emphasis on fresh, whole foods, healthy fats, and a balanced approach to eating makes it a valuable dietary choice for promoting health and vitality.

The Mediterranean diet is renowned for its numerous health benefits, as supported by various research findings. Here are some key insights from the search results:

1. **Reduced Risk of Chronic Diseases:** The Mediterranean diet has been associated with a reduced risk of developing heart disease, cancer, and type 2 diabetes. By following this diet, individuals may lower their risk of death at any age by 20% and protect against type 2 diabetes, thanks to its rich fiber content that aids in maintaining a healthy weight.

2. **Heart Health:** Studies have linked the Mediterranean diet with lower risk factors for heart disease, such as high cholesterol and high blood pressure. It is recognized as a healthy eating pattern by American nutrition experts and the World Health Organization .

3. **Longevity and Weight Management:** Embracing the Mediterranean diet has been shown to increase longevity and may help prevent weight gain. Additionally, it has been associated with a reduced risk of cognitive decline and may contribute to healthy aging.

4. **Overall Health Benefits:** The Mediterranean diet has been named the top diet by U.S. News & World Report for several consecutive years. It is praised for its potential health benefits, including its preventive effect toward cardiovascular diseases, decreased risk of diabetes and metabolic-related conditions, and potential role in preventing certain cancers .

In conclusion, the Mediterranean diet offers a wide range of health benefits, including reduced risk of chronic diseases, improved heart health, longevity, weight management, and overall well-being. Its emphasis on fresh, whole foods, healthy fats, and a balanced approach to eating makes it a valuable dietary choice for promoting health and vitality.

CHAPTER 1
BREAKFAST

FIG AND RICOTTA CROSTINI

Total Cooking Time: 15 minutes
Prep Time: 10 minutes
Servings: 4 (6 crostini per serving)

Ingredients:

- A French baguette, cut into slices that are 1/2-inch thick
- 1 container of ricotta cheese, measuring 15 ounces
- 12 basil leaves, thinly sliced
- 8 black mission figs, cut into quarters
- 1/4 cupagedbalsamicvinegar

Directions:

1. Change the oven temperature to 375°F (190°C) and wait for an adequate amount of time for it to reach the desired preheating temperature.
2. Position the baguette slices on a baking sheet that is covered with foil, ensuring that no greasing is required.
3. Put the bread into the oven that has been preheated and bake it until the bottoms become brown, which usually takes around 5 minutes. Flip the bread and continue baking for an additional 5 minutes until it becomes crisp. At last, take out the baking pan from the oven.
4. Apply 1 tablespoon of ricotta cheese evenly on top of each piece of toasted bread.
5. Place a basil leaf on top of the ricotta on each crostini.
6. Arrange 2 quarters of fig on each crostini.
7. Apply 1 tablespoon of ricotta cheese evenly on top of each piece of toasted bread.
8. Serve the fig and ricotta crostini immediately and enjoy!

Nutritional breakdown per serving:

Calories: 290 kcal, Protein: 10 grams, Carbohydrates: 51 grams, Fat: 6 grams, Saturated Fat: 6 grams, Cholesterol: 20 milligrams, Sodium: 360 milligrams, Fiber: 4 grams, and Sugar: 13 grams.

DELICIOUS AVOCADO TOAST WITH OLIVE OIL DRIZZLE AND A HINT OF ZA'ATAR

Total Cooking Time: 5 minutes
Prep Time: 3 minutes
Servings: 1 slice

Ingredients:

- 1 smallripeavocado
- 1 teaspoonfreshlemonjuice
- 1/2 teaspoonKoshersalt
- 1/2 teaspoonfreshlygroundblackpepper
- 1 slicewholegrainbread, toasted
- 1 teaspoonextra-virginoliveoil
- Za'atarseasoning
- Optional: Maldon sea salt flakes or red pepper flakes for garnish

Directions:

1. In a small bowl, combine the ripe avocado, lemon juice, salt, and pepper. Using a fork, gently mash the avocado until it reaches a smooth and creamy consistency.
2. Spread the mashed avocado mixture evenly on the toasted bread.
3. Carefully pour a drizzle of extra-virgin olive oil over the avocado toast.
4. Sprinkle Za'atar seasoning over the top of the avocado toast.
5. Optionally, garnish with Maldon sea salt flakes or red pepper flakes for added flavor.
6. Serve immediately and relish the delightful flavors!

Nutritional breakdown per serving:

Calories: 200 kcal, Protein: 5 grams, Carbohydrates: 18 grams, Fat: 13 grams, Saturated Fat: 3 grams, Cholesterol: 5 milligrams, Sodium: 415 milligrams, Fiber: 8 grams, and Sugar: 0 grams.

OMELETTE WITH SPINACH, FETA, AND TOMATOES

Total Cooking Time: 10 minutes
Prep Time: 5 minutes
Servings: 2 servings

Ingredients:

- 4 largeeggs
- 2 cupsfreshspinach
- 1 cupgrapetomatoes, halved
- 1/2 cupcrumbledfetacheese
- 2 tspextravirginoliveoil
- 1 tspdriedoregano
- Saltandpeppertotaste

Directions:

1. To commence, position a non-stick skillet on the stovetop over medium heat and drizzle 1 tablespoon of olive oil into it.
2. Add the spinach and sauté until wilted, about 2 minutes
3. In a mixing bowl, vigorously whisk the eggs while adding a pinch of salt, a dash of pepper, and a sprinkle of dried oregano for seasoning.
4. Pour the whisked eggs over the spinach in the skillet.
5. Sprinkle the halved grape tomatoes and crumbled feta cheese evenly over the eggs.
6. Cook for 3-4 minutes or until the omelette is set and the bottom is golden brown.
7. With the help of a spatula, carefully fold the omelette in half and delicately transfer it onto a plate.
8. Serve while hot and savor the delightful flavors!

Nutritional breakdown per serving:

Calories: 220 kcal, Protein: 16 grams, Carbohydrates: 6 grams, Fat: 15 grams, Saturated Fat: 4 grams, Cholesterol: 380 milligrams, Sodium: 500 milligrams, Fiber: 5 grams, and Sugar: 2 grams.

SHAKSHUKA (EGGS POACHED IN SPICY TOMATO SAUCE)

Total Cooking Time: 15 minutes
Prep Time: 10 minutes
Servings: 4-6 servings

Ingredients:

- 2 tbspoliveoil
- 1 largeyellowonion, diced
- 1 large red bell pepper, chopped
- 1 teaspoonfineseasalt
- 3 clovesgarlic, pressedorminced
- 2 tablespoonstomatopaste
- 1 teaspoongroundcumin
- 1 teaspoonsmokedpaprika
- 1/2 tsp red pepper flakes (adjust as desired)
- 1 can (28 ounces) whole or diced tomatoes, with their juices
- 6-8 largeeggs
- Salt and black pepper to taste
- Freshparsley, chopped, forgarnish
- Crusty bread, pita, or baguette for serving

Directions:

1. To begin cooking, heat the olive oil in a large skillet over medium heat. Then, proceed by adding the chopped onion and bell pepper to the skillet. Cook the vegetables until they are tender, which should take around 5 to 7 minutes.
2. Add the garlic, tomato paste, cumin, smoked paprika, and red pepper flakes. Stirandcookfor 1 minute.
3. Transfer the contents of the canned tomatoes, along with their juices, into the skillet. Proceed to break them up using a wooden spoon. Continue to let the sauce simmer over low heat for 10-15 minutes, stirring occasionally, until it achieves a slightly thicker consistency.

4. With a spoon, create small depressions in the sauce and delicately crack the eggs into the depressions. Gently sprinkle a small amount of salt and black pepper to elevate the taste of the eggs.

5. Place the lid on the skillet, allowing the eggs to gently simmer in the sauce for approximately 5 to 8 minutes. By following this method, you can ensure that the egg whites are thoroughly cooked, while the yolks retain their desired soft and tender consistency.

6. Once the eggs are cooked to your liking, remove the skillet from the heat. Garnishwithchoppedparsley.

7. Serve the shakshuka directly from the skillet with crusty bread, pita, or baguette for dipping.

Nutritional breakdown per serving:

Calories: 220 kcal, Protein: 16 grams, Carbohydrates: 6 grams, Fat: 15 grams, Saturated Fat: 3 grams, Cholesterol: 380 milligrams, Sodium: 450 milligrams, Fiber: 6 grams, and Sugar: 8 grams.

FIG AND RICOTTA TOAST WITH A DRIZZLE OF HONEY

Total Cooking Time: 5 minutes
Prep Time: 5 minutes
Servings: 1-2 servings

Ingredients:

- 2 slices of whole grain bread, toasted
- 1/2 cupricottacheese
- 4 ripefigs, sliced
- 2 tablespoonshoney
- Fresh mint leaves for garnish (optional)

Directions:

1. Toast the bread until it reaches a delightful golden brown color and achieves a satisfying crispiness.
2. Apply a generous amount of ricotta cheese onto each piece of toasted bread, ensuring an even and ample coating.
3. Arrange the sliced figs on top of the ricotta.
4. Drizzle honey over the figs and ricotta.
5. Garnish with fresh mint leaves if desired.
6. Serve immediately and relish the exquisite flavors!

Nutritional breakdown per serving:

Calories: 250 kcal, Protein: 8 grams, Carbohydrates: 45 grams, Fat: 7 grams, Saturated Fat: 1 grams, Cholesterol: 20 milligrams, Sodium: 600 milligrams, Fiber: 5 grams, and Sugar: 16 grams.

HONEY NUT TARTLETS

Total Cooking Time: 10 minutes
Prep Time: 5 minutes
Servings: 4 servings

Ingredients:

- 4 large navel oranges
- 1/2 cup chopped almonds
- 1/4 cup orange flower water
- Optional: Confectioners sugar for dusting
- Optional: Chopped pistachios for garnish

Directions:

1. With the aid of a sharp knife, meticulously remove the peel from the oranges, ensuring they are completely bare and rounded. Proceed to slice the oranges into thin, delicate pieces.
2. Put the chopped almonds into a dry skillet and cook over medium heat until they turn a light golden color and release a pleasant fragrance. Let them cool down before moving forward.
3. Place the orange slices in an appealing arrangement on a serving platter.
4. Sprinkle the toasted almonds over the oranges.
5. Drizzle the orange flower water over the salad.
6. If desired, dust the salad with confectioners sugar and sprinkle with chopped pistachios for an extra touch of flavor and presentation.
7. Serve the Orange and Almond Salad immediately as a refreshing and palate-cleansing dessert or a light and healthy snack.

Nutritional breakdown per serving:

Calories: 150 kcal, Protein: 3 grams, Carbohydrates: 20 grams, Fat: 7 grams, Saturated Fat: 0.5 grams, Cholesterol: 20 milligrams, Sodium: 0 milligrams, Fiber: 5 grams, and Sugar: 14 grams.

GRILLED HALLOUMI CHEESE WITH CHERRY TOMATOES AND FRESH HERBS

Total Cooking Time: 15 minutes
Prep Time: 5 minutes
Servings: 4 servings

Ingredients:

- 8 ounceshalloumicheese
- 1 tbsp olive oil or spray
- 1 cupcherrytomatoes, halved
- Fresh herbs like basil, mint, or oregano for garnish
- Lemonwedgesforserving

Directions:

1. Initiate the heating process of a grill or grill pan over medium-high heat.
2. Slice the halloumi cheese into 1/2-inch thick slices.
3. Carefully coat each side of the halloumi slices with a light layer of olive oil or olive oil spray.
4. Place the halloumi slices on the grill and cook for 2-3 minutes on each side, or until grill marks appear and the cheese is softened.
5. While the halloumi is grilling, place the halved cherry tomatoes on the grill, cut side down. Grill for 1 2 minutes until slightly charred and softened.
6. Arrange the grilled halloumi and cherry tomatoes on a serving platter.
7. Enhance the presentation by adding a finishing touch of fresh herbs like basil, mint, or oregano.
8. Serve the grilled halloumi and cherry tomatoes with lemon wedges on the side.

Nutritional breakdown per serving:

Calories: 145 kcal, Protein: 9 grams, Carbohydrates: 3 grams, Fat: 11 grams, Saturated Fat: 5 grams, Cholesterol: 30 milligrams, Sodium: 262 milligrams, Fiber: 0 grams, and Sugar: 2 grams.

MEDITERRANEAN BREAKFAST WRAP WITH HUMMUS, CUCUMBER, AND OLIVES

Total Cooking Time: 10 minutes

Prep Time: 5 minutes

Servings: 4 wraps

Ingredients:

- 1 cup hummus
- 1 large cucumber, thinly sliced
- 1/2 cup pitted olives, sliced
- 4 large flour tortillas or whole wheat wraps
- Optional garnish: Fresh herbs (basil, mint, or oregano)

Directions:

1. Lay out the tortillas on a clean surface.
2. Spread approximately 1/4 cup of hummus evenly over each tortilla.
3. Arrange the thinly sliced cucumber and sliced olives on top of the hummus.
4. If desired, sprinkle with fresh herbs such as basil, mint, or oregano for added flavor and freshness.
5. Roll the tortillas tightly, ensuring that the fillings are securely held in place by folding in the sides as you proceed.
6. Cut the wraps diagonally in half and serve promptly.

Nutritional breakdown per serving:

Calories: 280 kcal, Protein: 8 grams, Carbohydrates: 35 grams, Fat: 12 grams, Saturated Fat: 2 grams, Cholesterol: 0 milligrams, Sodium: 680 milligrams, Fiber: 6 grams, and Sugar: 2 grams.

ORANGE AND ALMOND BREAKFAST COUSCOUS

Total Cooking Time: 15 minutes
Prep Time: 5 minutes
Servings: 4 servings

Ingredients:

- 1 cup (10 oz) couscous
- 1 cupwaterorbroth
- 1/4 teaspoonsalt
- 1 tablespoonbutter
- 1 tablespoonoliveoil
- Zestof 1 orange
- 1/4 cupslicedalmonds, toasted
- Fresh mint leaves for garnish (optional)

Directions:

1. Heat a medium-sized saucepan and bring the water (or broth), salt, butter, and olive oil to a boil.
2. Add the couscous to the saucepan, stir well, cover tightly with a lid, and take it off the heat. Let the couscous sit and steam for a duration of 5 minutes.
3. Take a fork and gently loosen the couscous, ensuring that any clumps are broken up.
4. Gently fold in the orange zest and toasted sliced almonds.
5. Garnish with fresh mint leaves if desired.
6. Serve the orange and almond breakfast couscous warm.

Nutritional breakdown per serving:

Calories: 226 kcal, Protein: 7 grams, Carbohydrates: 37 grams, Fat: 5 grams, Saturated Fat: 2 grams, Cholesterol: 15 milligrams, Sodium: 220 milligrams, Fiber: 2 grams, and Sugar: 0 grams.

QUICK GREEK BREAKFAST SALAD WITH CUCUMBERS, OLIVES, AND FETA

Total Cooking Time: 10 minutes
Prep Time: 5 minutes
Servings: 4 servings

Ingredients:

- 2 largecucumbers, sliced
- 1 cupcherrytomatoes, halved
- 1/2 cuppittedKalamataolives
- 1 cupcrumbledfetacheese
- Fresh mint leaves for garnish (optional)
- Oliveoil
- Lemonjuice
- Driedoregano
- Saltandpeppertotaste

Directions:

1. In a shallow salad bowl, toss the sliced cucumbers, cherry tomatoes, and Kalamata olives together.
2. Carefully pour olive oil and lemon juice onto the salad, ensuring it is evenly distributed.
3. Sprinkle with dried oregano, salt, and pepper.
4. Top the salad with crumbled feta cheese.
5. If preferred, you can add a finishing touch by placing fresh mint leaves on top of the dish.
6. Enjoy the Quick Greek Breakfast Salad with Cucumbers, Olives, and Feta.

Nutritional breakdown per serving:

Calories: 187 kcal, Protein: 5 grams, Carbohydrates: 8 grams, Fat: 16 grams, Saturated Fat: 5 grams, Cholesterol: 22 milligrams, Sodium: 347 milligrams, Fiber: 2 grams, and Sugar: 4 grams.

BAKED EGGS WITH SPINACH AND FETA

Total Cooking Time: 15 minutes

Prep Time: 5 minutes

Servings: 1 serving (recipe can be easily multiplied for more servings)

Ingredients:

- 3 teaspoonsoliveoil
- 3-4 cupsfreshspinach, washed
- 1 wholeegg
- 1 ouncecrumbledfeta
- Saltandpeppertotaste

Directions:

1. Change the oven temperature to 350°F (180°C) and wait for an adequate amount of time for it to reach the desired preheating temperature.
2. In a pan, warm up 1 teaspoon of olive oil and cook the fresh spinach over medium heat for approximately 2-3 minutes until it becomes wilted.
3. Transfer the sautéed spinach to a small baking dish.
4. Create a well in the center of the spinach and crack the egg into the well.
5. Sprinkle the crumbled feta over the egg and spinach.
6. Season with salt and pepper to taste.
7. Put the baking dish into the oven that has been preheated and bake for about 10-12 minutes, or until the egg whites are cooked through while the yolk remains slightly runny.
8. After baking, take it out of the oven and allow it to cool for a minute.
9. Serve the baked eggs with spinach and feta immediately.

Nutritional breakdown per serving:

Calories: 215 kcal, Protein: 13 grams, Carbohydrates: 3 grams, Fat: 17 grams, Saturated Fat: 5 grams, Cholesterol: 195 milligrams, Sodium: 330 milligrams, Fiber: 1 grams, and Sugar: 1 grams.

FRESH FRUIT SALAD WITH A MINT-LIME DRESSING

Total Cooking Time: 10 minutes

Prep Time: 5 minutes

Servings: 6 servings

Ingredients:

- 1 pineapple, ripe, peeled, and cut into bite-sized chunks
- 2 ripemangoes, peeledandchopped
- 2 cups grapes, sliced (if preferred)
- 2 cupsstrawberries, hulledandhalved
- 1 tablespoonhoney
- Juiceandzestof 2 limes
- 1 tablespoon finely diced fresh mint leaves

Directions:

1. Combine the diced pineapple, mangoes, grapes, and strawberries in a large bowl, ensuring they are well mixed.
2. In a separate small bowl, whisk together the honey, lime juice, lime zest, and finely diced fresh mint leaves to create the mint-lime dressing.
3. Pour the mint-lime dressing over the prepared fruit.
4. Gently toss the fruit and dressing together until the fruit is evenly coated.
5. To maintain the ideal freshness, it is important to tightly cover the bowl with plastic wrap or transfer the fruit salad to an airtight container before placing it in the refrigerator. This will help preserve its freshness until it is ready to be enjoyed. This will help maintain its quality until it is ready to be served.
6. Serve the fresh fruit salad with mint-lime dressing chilled.

Nutritional breakdown per serving:

Calories: 136 kcal, Protein: 2 grams, Carbohydrates: 36 grams, Fat: 0 grams, Saturated Fat: 0 grams, Cholesterol: 35 milligrams, Sodium: 108 milligrams, Fiber: 2 grams, and Sugar: 10 grams.

TURKISH STYLE BREAKFAST EGGS WITH GARLICKY YOGURT AND CHILI BUTTER

Total Cooking Time: 15 minutes
Prep Time: 10 minutes
Servings: 2 servings

Ingredients:

Yogurt Spread:

- 1 cup Greek yogurt, at room temperature
- 1 clovegarlic
- 1/2 teaspoonfreshlygroundblackpepper
- 1/2 teaspoonsalt, ortotaste
- 1 pinchcayennepepper
- 2 tablespoons of finely chopped fresh dill, or adjust to your preference

AleppoButter:

- 1/4 stickunsaltedbutter
- 1 tablespoonAleppopepper

PoachedEggs:

- 4 largeeggs
- 1 tablespoon white vinegar (for poaching water)

Directions:

1. In a bowl, mix the Greek yogurt, minced garlic, black pepper, salt, cayenne pepper, and finely chopped fresh dill. Set aside.
2. Carefully heat the unsalted butter in a small saucepan on low heat until it transforms into a liquid state.
3. Blend the Aleppo pepper into the butter, allowing it to impart its flavors. Set the mixture aside.
4. Add water to a spacious and deep skillet, then heat it gradually until it reaches a gentle simmer.

5. Add the white vinegar to the water.
6. Break each egg into an individual small bowl or ramekin.
7. Generate a mild whirlpool in the water and cautiously slip the eggs into the gently simmering water.
8. Allow the eggs to poach for approximately 3-4 minutes to achieve a soft yolk, or extend the cooking time for a firmer yolk.
9. Spread a thick layer of the garlicky yogurt with herbs on a serving plate or small bowl.
10. With a slotted spoon, carefully lift the poached eggs out of the water and place them on the yogurt base, ensuring a gentle and precise placement.
11. Drizzle the spiced Aleppo butter over the poached eggs and yogurt.
12. Garnish with additional fresh mint, dill, and black pepper if desired.
13. Serve the Turkish Style Breakfast Eggs with Garlicky Yogurt and Chili Butter immediately, accompanied by toasted crusty bread for dipping.

Nutritional breakdown per serving:

Calories: 320 kcal, Protein: 23 grams, Carbohydrates: 9 grams, Fat: 22 grams, Saturated Fat: 12 grams, Cholesterol: 430 milligrams, Sodium: 580 milligrams, Fiber: 1 grams, and Sugar: 6 grams.

HERBED FETA CHEESE AND TOMATO BRUSCHETTA

Total Cooking Time: 15 minutes
Prep Time: 15 minutes
Servings: 4 servings

Ingredients:

- 20-24 ounces fresh tomatoes, diced small
- 1/4 cupfreshbasil, choppedfinely
- 2 tablespoonsoliveoil
- 1 tablespoonredwinevinegar
- 1 clovegarlic, minced
- 1/2 teaspoonsalt, ortotaste
- 1/4 tsp of black pepper, adjust to your preference
- 1 baguette

Directions:

1. Mix the diced tomatoes, basil, garlic, olive oil, red wine vinegar, salt, and black pepper together in a bowl. Make sure all the ingredients are evenly combined. Set the mixture aside to be used later.
2. Slice the baguette into 1/4" thick pieces on the bias.
3. Change the oven temperature to 375°F (190°C) and wait until it reaches the desired preheating level.
4. Position the baguette slices on a baking sheet and delicately apply a thin layer of olive oil using a brush.
5. Place the bread in the preheated oven and toast it for approximately 5 to 7 minutes, or until it turns a golden brown color and becomes crispy.
6. Gently rub the warm toasted bread with a single raw garlic clove.
7. Spoon the prepared tomato mixture over the toasted bread.
8. Serve the herbed feta cheese and tomato bruschetta immediately, optionally garnished with fresh basil leaves.

Nutritional breakdown per serving:

Calories: 179 kcal, Protein: 3 grams, Carbohydrates: 25 grams, Fat: 7 grams, Saturated Fat: 1 grams, Cholesterol: 0 milligrams, Sodium: 263 milligrams, Fiber: 3 grams, and Sugar: 5 grams.

MEDITERRANEAN BREAKFAST BURRITO WITH SCRAMBLED EGGS, FETA, AND SPINACH

Total Cooking Time: 15 minutes
Prep Time: 10 minutes
Servings: 4 servings

Ingredients:

- 8 largeeggs
- 1 tablespoonoliveoil
- 2 cupsfreshspinach, chopped
- 1/2 cupcrumbledfetacheese
- 1/4 teaspoonsalt
- 1/4 teaspoonblackpepper
- 4 largewholewheattortillas

Directions:

1. Place the eggs in a bowl and vigorously whisk them until they are completely mixed and well incorporated.
2. To start, place the skillet over medium heat and heat the olive oil until it reaches the desired temperature.
3. Next, include the diced spinach in the skillet and cook for approximately 2-3 minutes until it becomes wilted.
4. Afterward, carefully pour the beaten eggs over the wilted spinach in the skillet and cook while gently stirring until the eggs are fully scrambled and cooked through.
5. Warm the tortillas slightly to make them pliable.
6. Divide the scrambled eggs and spinach mixture evenly among the tortillas.
7. Sprinkle the crumbled feta cheese over the scrambled eggs in each tortilla.
8. Lastly, add salt and black pepper according to your personal preference for seasoning.
9. Gently fold the sides of the tortillas over the filling and tightly roll them up, ensuring to tuck in the edges as you proceed.
10. Serve the Mediterranean Breakfast Burritos with Scrambled Eggs, Feta, and Spinach immediately, optionally accompanied by a side of salsa or a light salad.

Nutritional breakdown per serving:

Calories: 320 kcal, Protein: 20 grams, Carbohydrates: 23 grams, Fat: 18 grams, Saturated Fat: 6 grams, Cholesterol: 380 milligrams, Sodium: 620 milligrams, Fiber: 4 grams, and Sugar: 2 grams.

EGG AND HUMMUS BREAKFAST SANDWICH WITH ARUGULA AND CHERRY TOMATOES

Total Cooking Time: 15 minutes
Prep Time: 10 minutes
Servings: 2-4 servings

Ingredients:

For the Sandwich:

- 4 slicesofwholegrainbread
- 4 largeeggs
- 1 cuparugula
- 1 tablespoonoliveoil
- 1 teaspoonfreshlemonjuice
- Saltandpeppertotaste
- Cookingspray

FortheHummusSpread:

- 1/2 cuphummus

Directions:

1. Spread a generous amount of hummus on one side of each slice of whole grain bread.
2. To get started, warm up the olive oil in a frying pan over medium heat.
3. Delicately crack the eggs into the frying pan and cook them to your preferred degree of doneness, enhancing their taste with a dash of salt and pepper.
4. Place a generous handful of arugula onto the bread slices, spreading them with a layer of hummus.
5. Carefully place a cooked egg on top of the arugula on two of the bread slices.
6. Drizzle the eggs with fresh lemon juice.
7. Cover the assembled sandwiches by placing the remaining bread slices on top.
8. Serve the Egg and Hummus Breakfast Sandwiches with Arugula and Cherry Tomatoes immediately.

Nutritional breakdown per serving:

Calories: 320 kcal, Protein: 18 grams, Carbohydrates: 30 grams, Fat: 15 grams, Saturated Fat: 3 grams, Cholesterol: 370 milligrams, Sodium: 540 milligrams, Fiber: 5 grams, and Sugar: 3 grams.

SPINACH & FETA SCRAMBLED EGG PITAS

Total Cooking Time: 15 minutes
Prep Time: 5-10 minutes
Servings: 2-4 servings

Ingredients:

For the Spinach & Feta Scrambled Egg Pitas:

- 8 largeeggs
- 1 cup of thawed and drained frozen chopped spinach
- 1/2 cupcrumbledfetacheese
- 4 whole-wheatpitas
- 2 tablespoons sun-dried tomato tapenade or basil pesto
- Saltandpeppertotaste

Directions:

1. Combine the eggs in a bowl, ensuring they are thoroughly mixed.
2. In a non-stick skillet, cook the eggs over medium heat, stirring gently, until they are scrambled and fully cooked.
3. Include the thawed and drained chopped spinach into the scrambled eggs and cook for an extra 1-2 minutes to let the flavors blend together.
4. Mix in the crumbled feta cheese and tailor the seasoning with salt and pepper to complement your unique taste preferences.
5. Lightly toast the whole-wheat pitas to warm them.
6. Spread a layer of sun-dried tomato tapenade or basil pesto on each pita.
7. Divide the spinach and feta scrambled eggs evenly among the pitas, spooning the mixture into each pita pocket.
8. Serve the Spinach & Feta Scrambled Egg Pitas immediately, optionally accompanied by a side salad or fresh fruit.

Nutritional breakdown per serving:

Calories: 320 kcal, Protein: 20 grams, Carbohydrates: 23 grams, Fat: 18 grams, Saturated Fat: 7 grams, Cholesterol: 380 milligrams, Sodium: 620 milligrams, Fiber: 4 grams, and Sugar: 2 grams.

BREAKFAST SALAD WITH EGG & SALSA VERDE VINAIGRETTE

Total Cooking Time: 15 minutes
Prep Time: 5-8 minutes
Servings: 1 serving

Ingredients:

For the Salad:

- 3 cups mixed greens (such as spinach, arugula, or kale)
- 1 largeegg
- 2 tablespoonssalsaverde
- 1 teaspoonextra-virginoliveoil
- Additional cilantro for garnish (optional)

Directions:

1. In a large bowl, mix together the mixed greens, 1 tablespoon of salsa verde, and 1 teaspoon of olive oil. Toss the ingredients together until the greens are evenly coated.
2. Using medium-high heat, heat up a small nonstick skillet with 1 teaspoon of olive oil until it is warm.
3. Using medium-high heat, heat up 1 teaspoon of olive oil in a small nonstick skillet.
4. Place the dressed mixed greens on a serving plate.
5. Carefully place the fried egg on top of the salad.
6. Drizzle the remaining salsa verde vinaigrette over the salad and egg.
7. If you would like, you have the option to enhance the dish by adding a sprinkle of cilantro as a garnish just before serving without delay.

Nutritional breakdown per serving:

Calories: 527 kcal, Protein: 16 grams, Carbohydrates: 37 grams, Fat: 34 grams, Saturated Fat: 5 grams, Cholesterol: 186 milligrams, Sodium: 660 milligrams, Fiber: 13 grams, and Sugar: 2 grams.

EGG SALAD AVOCADO TOAST

Total Cooking Time: 5 minutes
Prep Time: 5 minutes
Servings: 1 serving

Ingredients:

- 1 ripeavocado
- 1 tablespoonchoppedcelery
- 1 teaspoonlemonjuice
- 1/4 teaspoonhotsauce
- Pinchofsalt
- 1 hard-boiledegg, chopped
- 1 slicewhole-wheattoast

Directions:

1. Take a small bowl and combine the mashed ripe avocado with diced celery, lemon juice, hot sauce, and a pinch of salt. Mix thoroughly until all the ingredients are well blended.
2. Add the chopped hard-boiled egg to the avocado mixture and gently mix until the egg is evenly distributed.
3. Spread the avocado and egg mixture onto the whole-wheat toast.
4. Serve the Egg Salad Avocado Toast immediately for a quick and satisfying meal.

Nutritional breakdown per serving:

Calories: 271 kcal, Protein: 12 grams, Carbohydrates: 18 grams, Fat: 18 grams, Saturated Fat: 4 grams, Cholesterol: 186 milligrams, Sodium: 216 milligrams, Fiber: 5 grams, and Sugar: 2 grams.

REALLY GREEN SMOOTHIE

Total Cooking Time: 5 minutes
Prep Time: 5 minutes
Servings: 1 serving

Ingredients:

- 1 cupkaleorspinach
- 1/2 ripeavocado
- 1/2 cupchoppedcucumber
- 1/2 cupchoppedpineapple
- 1/2 cupcoconutwaterorwater
- 1 tablespoonfreshlemonjuice
- Optional: 1 tablespoon chia seeds or flaxseeds

Directions:

1. In a blender, combine the kale or spinach, ripe avocado, chopped cucumber, chopped pineapple, coconut water or water, and fresh lemon juice.
2. Optionally, add chia seeds or flaxseeds for an extra nutritional boost.
3. Using a blender, combine the ingredients until a smooth and well-blended mixture is achieved. If necessary, add additional liquid to achieve the desired consistency.
4. Pour the Really Green Smoothie into a glass and enjoy immediately for a refreshing and nutrient-packed drink.

Nutritional breakdown per serving:

Calories: 210 kcal, Protein: 5 grams, Carbohydrates: 28 grams, Fat: 11 grams, Saturated Fat: 1.5 grams, Cholesterol: 0 milligrams, Sodium: 50 milligrams, Fiber: 10 grams, and Sugar: 5 grams.

CHAPTER 2
SMALL PLATES
AND SNACKS

HUMMUS WITH WARM PITA BREAD

Total Cooking Time: 15 minutes
Prep Time: 10 minutes
Servings: 4 servings

Ingredients

- 2 (15-ounce) cans chickpeas, drained and rinsed
- 3 tablespoonsoliveoil
- 2 tablespoonslemonjuice
- 2 clovesgarlic, minced
- 1 teaspoongroundcumin
- Salttotaste
- Warmpitabreadforserving

DetailedDirections

1. Combine chickpeas, olive oil, lemon juice, minced garlic, ground cumin, and a pinch of salt in a food processor. Continue processing the mixture until it reaches a smooth and cohesive texture, ensuring that all the ingredients are fully combined.

2. Keep blending the mixture until it achieves a smooth and creamy texture. Remember to scrape the sides of the bowl to ensure that all the ingredients are well combined and evenly blended.

3. If the hummus seems too thick, you can slowly incorporate small quantities of water or additional olive oil, adding one tablespoon at a time, until you reach the desired consistency.

4. Take a moment to taste the hummus and make any necessary adjustments to the seasoning. Feel at liberty to incorporate additional salt or lemon juice based on your individual taste and preference.

5. Warm the pita bread in the oven or on a grill for a few minutes until heated through.

6. Serve the creamy hummus with warm pita bread for dipping.

Nutritional breakdown per serving:

Calories: 200 kcal, Protein: 7 grams, Carbohydrates: 20 grams, Fat: 10 grams, Saturated Fat: 1 grams, Cholesterol: 57 milligrams, Sodium: 158 milligrams, Fiber: 4 grams, and Sugar: 3 grams.

MARINATED OLIVES WITH HERBS AND CITRUS ZEST

Total Cooking Time: 5-15 minutes
Prep Time: 5 minutes
Servings: 4-6 servings

Ingredients:

- 2 cups mixed olives (such as Kalamata, green, and black olives)
- Zestof 1 lemon
- Zestof 1 orange
- 2 clovesgarlic, minced
- 2 tablespoonsextra-virginoliveoil
- 1 tablespoonfreshlemonjuice
- 1 tablespoonfreshorangejuice
- 1 teaspoondriedoregano
- 1/2 teaspoon red pepper flakes
- Top it off with fresh herbs like thyme, rosemary, or basil

Directions:

1. In a bowl, combine the mixed olives, lemon zest, orange zest, minced garlic, extra-virgin olive oil, lemon juice, orange juice, dried oregano, and red pepper flakes. Mix well to ensure the olives are coated with the marinade.
2. Place a cover on the bowl and refrigerate the olives for a minimum of 2 hours, or ideally overnight. This will enable the flavors to blend and penetrate the olives.
3. Before serving, remove the marinated olives from the refrigerator and let them come to room temperature for about 15 minutes.
4. Place the olives into a serving dish, sprinkle some fresh herbs on top for garnish, and serve.
5. These marinated olives can be enjoyed as a standalone appetizer or served alongside a cheese platter, charcuterie board, or as part of a Mediterranean-inspired meal.

Nutritional breakdown per serving:

Calories: 244 kcal, Protein: 24 grams, Carbohydrates: 12 grams, Fat: 18 grams, Saturated Fat: 3 grams, Cholesterol: 4 milligrams, Sodium: 978 milligrams, Fiber: 7 grams, and Sugar: 0 grams.

TZATZIKI WITH CRUDITES FOR DIPPING

Total Cooking Time: 10 minutes

Prep Time: 10 minutes

Servings: 4 to 6 servings

Ingredients

- 3 Persiancucumbers
- 2 cups plain whole-milk Greek yogurt
- 2 tablespoonsfinelychoppeddill
- 1 tablespoonlemonjuice
- 1 garlicclove, minced
- Saltandpeppertotaste

DetailedDirections

1. Grate the Persian cucumbers using the larger holes of a box grater. Squeeze the grated cucumbers to remove excess water, then place them in a medium bowl (you should have about 1 cup).
2. Combine the grated cucumbers, plain whole-milk Greek yogurt, finely chopped dill, lemon juice, minced garlic, and season with salt and pepper in the same bowl.
3. Thoroughly combine all the ingredients until they are well mixed.
4. You can choose to serve the Tzatziki right away, or for a bolder taste, cover and refrigerate it for a minimum of one hour to allow the flavors to meld together in perfect harmony.
5. Serve the Tzatziki with a variety of crudites for dipping, such as carrot sticks, cucumber slices, bell pepper strips, and cherry tomatoes.

Nutritional breakdown per serving:

Calories: 70 kcal, Protein2 24 grams, Carbohydrates: 4 grams, Fat: 0 grams, Saturated Fat: 3 grams, Cholesterol: 15 milligrams, Sodium: 130 milligrams, Fiber: 0 grams, and Sugar: 2 grams.

FETA AND WATERMELON SKEWERS WITH BALSAMIC GLAZE

Total Cooking Time: 15minutes

Prep Time: 15 minutes

Servings:20 skewers

Ingredients

- 1 small seedless watermelon, cut into bite-sized cubes
- 8 oz block of feta cheese, cut into bite-sized cubes
- Freshmintleavesforgarnish
- Balsamicglazeorreduction

DetailedDirections

1. Assemble the skewers by gently poking a feta cube followed by 1-2 watermelon cubes onto metal, plastic, or wooden skewers, toothpicks, or appetizer sticks, depending on preference and size.
2. Once all the skewers are filled, drizzle them with balsamic glaze or homemade balsamic reduction.
3. Add a fresh mint leaf as a garnish to each watermelon and feta skewer.
4. Enjoy the skewers immediately as a delightful and refreshing appetizer.

Nutritional breakdown per serving:

Calories: 200 kcal, Protein: 8 grams, Carbohydrates: 11 grams, Fat: 12 grams, Saturated Fat: 1 grams, Cholesterol: 30 milligrams, Sodium: 400 milligrams, Fiber: 2 grams, and Sugar: 8 grams.

ARTICHOKE AND WHITE BEAN DIP

Total Cooking Time: 10 minutes
Prep Time: 10 minutes
Servings: 8 servings

Ingredients:

- 14-ounce can white beans, rinsed and drained
- 1 cup artichoke hearts
- 3 tablespoons olive oil
- 5 cloves garlic
- Zest and juice of 1 lemon
- Salt and black pepper to taste
- If desired, you can add a garnish of fresh herbs like parsley, dill, or basil

Directions:

1. In a food processor or blender, combine the white beans, artichoke hearts, olive oil, garlic, lemon zest, and lemon juice. Process or blend the mixture until it becomes smooth and well blended.
2. Continue blending the ingredients until they reach a velvety smooth and creamy consistency. Take a small taste of the mixture and make any necessary adjustments to the flavor by adding salt and black pepper to your desired liking.
3. Spoon the dip into a shallow bowl and make a well in the center with the back of a spoon.
4. Drizzle a small amount of olive oil over the dip, and sprinkle a pinch of chili flakes on top to add a flavorful touch of heat.
5. Enhance the dip by adding a vibrant and aromatic touch with a garnish of fresh herbs, such as Italian parsley, dill, or basil.

Nutritional breakdown per serving:

Calories: 146 kcal, Protein: 6 grams, Carbohydrates: 14 grams, Fat: 9 grams, Saturated Fat: 2 grams, Cholesterol: 0 milligrams, Sodium: 418 milligrams, Fiber: 5 grams, and Sugar: 1 grams.

GRILLED HALLOUMI CHEESE WITH A DRIZZLE OF HONEY

Total Cooking Time: 10-15 minutes

Prep Time: 5 minutes

Servings: 4

Ingredients

- 1 block of halloumi cheese, sliced into 8 pieces
- Oliveoilforbrushing
- Honeyfordrizzling

DetailedDirections

1. Start by slicing the block of halloumi cheese into eight equal slices.
2. Brush the slices with olive oil to prevent sticking and to enhance the grilling process.
3. Begin by heating a grill pan over medium heat, ensuring it is properly preheated. Then, delicately place the halloumi slices onto the pan, taking care to position them evenly.
4. Grill the halloumi slices for 3-5 minutes on each side until they develop a golden brown color and grill marks.
5. Once grilled, remove the halloumi slices from the pan and place them on a serving platter.
6. Enhance the flavor of the grilled halloumi by generously drizzling it with honey, creating a delightful balance of sweet and savory tastes.
7. To fully savor the delectable flavors, serve the grilled halloumi promptly while it is still hot and enjoy the delightful taste experience.

Nutritional breakdown per serving:

Calories: 250 kcal, Protein: 18 grams, Carbohydrates: 2 grams, Fat: 20 grams, Saturated Fat: 3 grams, Cholesterol: 0 milligrams, Sodium: 500 milligrams, Fiber: 0 grams, and Sugar: 1 grams.

GRILLED SHRIMP SKEWERS

Total Cooking Time: 10 minutes

Prep Time: 10-15 minutes

Servings: 4-6

Ingredients:

- 1 pound large shrimp, peeled and deveined
- 3-4 clovesgarlic, minced
- 1/4 cupoliveoil
- 2 tablespoonsfreshlemonjuice
- 1 teaspoondriedoregano
- Saltandpeppertotaste
- Optional: Add a final touch by garnishing with fresh herbs such as parsley or cilantro.

Directions:

1. To make the marinade for the shrimp, combine minced garlic, olive oil, fresh lemon juice, dried oregano, salt, and pepper in a large bowl.
2. Ensure that the peeled and deveined shrimp are evenly coated by placing them into the marinade. Marinate for up to a couple of hours to allow the flavors to infuse, or prepare the marinade up to a day in advance to cut down further on prep time.
3. Skewer the marinated shrimp onto bamboo sticks or metal skewers.
4. Preheat the grill to medium-high heat.
5. Cook the shrimp skewers on the grill for approximately 2-3 minutes per side, or until they become opaque and obtain a pinkish-orange hue. It's important not to overcook the shrimp to maintain their juiciness and tenderness.
6. After cooking, take the shrimp skewers off the grill and optionally add a garnish of fresh herbs.

Nutritional breakdown per serving:

Calories: 342 kcal, Protein: 23 grams, Carbohydrates: 5 grams, Fat: 29 grams, Saturated Fat: 5 grams, Cholesterol: 0 milligrams, Sodium: 210 milligrams, Fiber: 2 grams, and Sugar: 3 grams.

CILANTRO-LIME HUMMUS

Total Cooking Time: 5 minutes
Prep Time: 5 minutes
Servings: 2 cups

Ingredients:

- 1 (15 ounce) cangarbanzobeans, drained
- 1 cupfreshcilantro
- 1 jalapeñopepper, stemmedanddiced
- 2 clovesgarlic, diced
- 1 tablespoonoliveoil
- Salt and ground black pepper to taste
- 1 pinchgarlicpowder
- Zestandjuiceof 1 lime

Directions:

1. Combine the drained garbanzo beans, fresh cilantro, diced jalapeño pepper, diced garlic, olive oil, salt, black pepper, garlic powder, and the zest and juice of one lime in a food processor.
2. Continue pulsing the mixture until a smooth and uniform consistency is achieved, ensuring that all the ingredients are thoroughly blended and evenly incorporated.
3. Blend the ingredients until smooth, adjusting the seasonings to taste.
4. If a smoother texture is desired, additional olive oil can be added, as suggested by one of the sources.
5. Transfer the cilantro-lime hummus to a serving bowl.

Nutritional breakdown per serving:

Calories: 171 kcal, Protein: 6 grams, Carbohydrates: 19 grams, Fat: 9 grams, Saturated Fat: 1 grams, Cholesterol: 0 milligrams, Sodium: 367 milligrams, Fiber: 5 grams, and Sugar: 3 grams.

ROASTED RED PEPPER AND FETA DIP WITH PITA CHIPS

Total Cooking Time 5-15 minutes
Prep Time: 5 to 15 minutes
Servings: 6 - 12 servings

Ingredients:

- 8 ounces feta cheese, patted dry and crumbled
- 1/2 cup of roasted red peppers that have been dried and roughly chopped
- 1/4 cup of extra-virgin olive oil to the mixture, and reserve some extra for garnishing
- 1 tablespoonlemonjuice
- 1/4 teaspoon cayenne pepper
- Freshly ground black pepper, to taste
- Crushed red pepper flakes, for garnish (optional)
- Pitachips, forserving

Directions:

1. In a food processor, combine the crumbled feta cheese, roasted red peppers, extra-virgin olive oil, lemon juice, cayenne pepper (if using), and freshly ground black pepper. Processuntilsmoothandcreamy.
2. Sample the dip and modify the seasoning by adding more lemon juice, black pepper, or cayenne pepper to your liking.
3. Place the dip into a bowl for serving. Decorate it by drizzling some extra-virgin olive oil and sprinkling crushed red pepper flakes on top.
4. Accompany the Roasted Red Pepper and Feta Dip with pita chips or the dippers of your choice when serving.

Nutritional breakdown per serving:

Calories: 250 kcal, Protein: 11 grams, Carbohydrates: 5 grams, Fat: 30 grams, Saturated Fat: 9 grams, Cholesterol: 15 milligrams, Sodium: 1258 milligrams, Fiber: 4 grams, and Sugar: 3 grams.

MARINATED FETA CUBES

Total Cooking Time: 10 minutes
Prep Time: 10 minutes
Servings: 8-10 servings

Ingredients:

- 8 ounces creamy feta in the brine
- Extravirginoliveoil
- 1 jalapeño, thinlysliced
- 3 to 4 drychilies
- 1 to 2 teaspoonsdriedoregano
- 2 to 3 tablespoonschoppedparsley
- Zestof 1 lemon

Directions:

1. Cut the feta cheese into large cubes and arrange them inside a mason jar or a container with an airtight seal.
2. In a compact bowl, mix together 1/2 cup of high-quality olive oil with finely sliced jalapeño, dried chilies, oregano, parsley, and lemon zest.
3. Delicately drizzle the olive oil mixture over the feta cubes, ensuring they are fully immersed in the fragrant combination of oil and herbs.
4. Seal the jar tightly and refrigerate the marinated feta for at least 24 hours to allow the flavors to infuse. For best results, marinate the feta for up to one week to achieve optimal flavor.

Nutritional breakdown per serving:

Calories: 501 kcal, Protein: 10 grams, Carbohydrates: 5 grams, Fat: 45 grams, Saturated Fat: 15 grams, Cholesterol: 25 milligrams, Sodium: 367 milligrams, Fiber: 8 grams, and Sugar: 4 grams.

STUFFED MINI TOMATOES

Total Cooking Time: 20 minutes
Prep Time: 15 minutes
Servings: 12 servings

Ingredients:

- 24 cherryorgrapetomatoes
- 8 oz. creamcheese, softened
- 1/4 cup finely chopped fresh herbs
- Salt and pepper to taste
- Optional toppings: chopped olives, crispy bacon bits, or finely chopped nuts

Directions:

1. Wash and dry the cherry or grape tomatoes. Slice off the top of each tomato and carefully scoop out the seeds and pulp to create a hollow cavity.
2. In a bowl, blend together the cream cheese, finely chopped fresh herbs, salt, and pepper until thoroughly mixed.
3. With the help of a small spoon or a piping bag, meticulously fill each hollowed tomato with the irresistible blend of cream cheese infused with aromatic herbs.
4. Optional: Top the stuffed tomatoes with chopped olives, crispy bacon bits, or finely chopped nuts for added flavor and texture.
5. Arrange the filled miniature tomatoes on a decorative platter and place in the refrigerator until you're ready to present them.

Nutritional breakdown per serving:

Calories: 32 kcal, Protein: 2 grams, Carbohydrates: 7 grams, Fat: 1 grams, Saturated Fat: 0 grams, Cholesterol: 0 milligrams, Sodium: 52 milligrams, Fiber: 3 grams, and Sugar: 5 grams.

CUCUMBER AND TOMATO SALAD

Total Cooking Time: 15 minutes
Prep Time: 15 minutes
Servings: 4 servings

Ingredients:

- 1 longEnglishcucumber, sliced
- 2-3 largetomatoes, diced
- 1 redonion, sliced
- 1 tablespoon fresh herbs, optional
- 2 tablespoonsoliveoil
- 1 tablespoonredwinevinegar
- Saltandpeppertotaste

Directions:

1. In a spacious bowl, mix together the sliced cucumber, diced tomatoes, sliced red onion, and fresh herbs (if desired).
2. Carefully drizzle the olive oil and red wine vinegar over the salad ingredients.
3. Modify the flavor with salt and pepper to complement your distinct taste preferences.
4. Toss the salad well to ensure the ingredients are evenly coated with the dressing.
5. Chill the cucumber and tomato salad in the refrigerator for a minimum of 15 minutes prior to serving, allowing the flavors to blend together harmoniously.

Nutritional breakdown per serving:

Calories: 90 kcal, Protein: 2 grams, Carbohydrates: 5 grams, Fat: 8 grams, Saturated Fat: 2.5 grams, Cholesterol: 5 milligrams, Sodium: 120 milligrams, Fiber: 1 grams, and Sugar: 2 grams.

TZATZIKI DIP

Total Cooking Time: 15 minutes
Prep Time: 15 minutes
Servings: 2 cups

Ingredients:

- 2 cups grated cucumber
- 1.5 cupsofGreekyogurt
- 2 tbsp extra-virgin olive oil
- 2 tbsp fresh mint and/or dill (chopped)
- 1 tablespoonlemonjuice
- 1 medium clove garlic, pressed or minced
- 1/2 teaspoonfineseasalt

Directions:

1. To prepare the cucumber, grate it using the larger holes of a box grater.
2. In a mixing bowl, combine the grated cucumber, plain Greek yogurt, extra-virgin olive oil, chopped fresh mint and/or dill, lemon juice, pressed or minced garlic, and fine sea salt.
3. Stir the ingredients until well combined.
4. For optimal flavor, it is advised to refrigerate the Tzatziki dip for a minimum of 1 hour before serving. This will enable the flavors to merge, resulting in a pleasurable and well-balanced taste sensation.

Nutritional breakdown per serving:

Calories: 84 kcal, Protein: 2 grams, Carbohydrates: 2 grams, Fat: 3 grams, Saturated Fat: 0 grams, Cholesterol: 0 milligrams, Sodium: 25 milligrams, Fiber: 2 grams, and Sugar: 2 grams.

MINI GREEK SALAD SKEWERS WITH CUCUMBER, TOMATOES, AND FETA

Total Cooking Time 15 minutes

Prep Time: 10-15 minutes

Servings: 6-12servings

Ingredients

- 12 cherrytomatoes
- 6 (1/2 inch) cucumberslices, halved
- 12 (1 by 1/2 inch) pieces of red onion
- 12 (1/2 inch) cubes of feta cheese (3 ounces)
- 12 Kalamataolives
- 1/3 cup Greek salad dressing (refer to associated recipe)

DetailedDirections

1. Serve the Mini Greek Salad Skewers alongside a side of Greek salad dressing, perfect for dipping or drizzling.
2. Repeat the process until you have assembled 12 skewers.
3. Serve the Mini Greek Salad Skewers alongside a side of Greek salad dressing, perfect for dipping or drizzling.

Nutritional breakdown per serving:

Calories: 60 kcal, Protein: 3 grams, Carbohydrates: 4 grams, Fat: 4 grams, Saturated Fat: 2 grams, Cholesterol: 10 milligrams, Sodium: 100 milligrams, Fiber: 1 grams, and Sugar: 2 grams.

GRILLED SHRIMP WITH LEMON AND GARLIC

Total Cooking Time: 10-15 minutes
Prep Time: 5-10 minutes
Servings: 4-6 servings

Ingredients:

- 1 pound large shrimp, peeled and deveined
- 2 tablespoonsoliveoil
- 4 clovesgarlic, minced
- Zestof 1 lemon
- Juiceof 1 lemon
- Saltandpepper, totaste
- Fresh parsley, chopped (for garnish)

Directions:

1. Preheat the grill to medium-high heat.

2. In a mixing bowl, thoroughly blend together olive oil, minced garlic, lemon zest, lemon juice, salt, and pepper until the ingredients are fully combined.

3. Transfer the shrimp to the bowl and delicately toss them until they are uniformly coated with the marinade.

4. Skewer the shrimp, ensuring there is some space left between each piece.

5. Position the shrimp skewers on the preheated grill and grill them for approximately 2-3 minutes per side, or until the shrimp turn opaque and are fully cooked.

6. Take the shrimp skewers off the grill and move them to a platter for serving.

7. Decorate the dish with freshly chopped parsley as a garnish and serve promptly.

Nutritional breakdown per serving:

Calories: 220 kcal, Protein: 15 grams, Carbohydrates: 1 grams, Fat: 16 grams, Saturated Fat: 3 grams, Cholesterol: 150 milligrams, Sodium: 650 milligrams, Fiber: 2 grams, and Sugar: 2 grams.

MARINATED ARTICHOKE HEARTS

Total Cooking Time: 15 minutes
Prep Time: 10 minutes
Servings: 3 servings

Ingredients:

- 1 lemon, juiced
- 2 tablespoonsextra-virginoliveoil
- 2 clovesgarlic, chopped (Optional)
- 1 teaspoonItalianseasoning
- 1 tsp salt, or as desired
- 1 tspblackpepper, totaste
- 1 (14 oz) can artichoke hearts, drained

Directions:

1. In a jar, mix lemon juice, olive oil, garlic (optional), Italian seasoning, salt, and pepper.
2. Seal the jar and shake the ingredients until well combined.
3. Add the drained quartered artichoke hearts to the jar and seal it.
4. Shake the jar to ensure the artichoke hearts are coated with the marinade.
5. Allow the marinated artichoke hearts to rest for at least 10 minutes to absorb the flavors before serving

Nutritional breakdown per serving:

Calories: 130 kcal, Protein: 2 grams, Carbohydrates: 5 grams, Fat: 4 grams, Saturated Fat: 1 grams, Cholesterol: 2 milligrams, Sodium: 240 milligrams, Fiber: 3 grams, and Sugar: 0 grams.

ARTICHOKE AND OLIVE TAPENADE WITH CROSTINI

Total Cooking Time: 15
Prep Time: 10-15 minutes
Servings: 4-12 servings

Ingredients

- 14 ozcannedartichokehearts, drained
- 2-4 cloves garlic, peeled and rough chopped
- 1/2 cupKalamataolives, drained
- 2 tablespoonscapers, drained
- 1/2 cup fresh parsley, chopped and separated
- 1 tablespoonfreshlemonjuice
- 4 tablespoons olive oil, plus 2-3 tablespoons for brushing
- 1/4 tsp sea salt, with an additional pinch for enhancing the dish's appearance
- 1/8 teaspoon red pepper flakes (optional)
- 1/4 cup shredded Parmesan cheese (optional)
- Baguette

DetailedDirections

1. Preheat the oven to 350°F. Line a sheet pan with parchment paper.
2. In a food processor, add the artichokes, garlic, Kalamata olives, capers, half of the chopped parsley, lemon juice, 4 tablespoons of olive oil, sea salt, and red pepper flakes (if using). Process the ingredients until they are finely chopped and well mixed, but not completely pureed. Transfer the mixture to a spacious mixing bowl.
3. Slice the baguette into thin pieces and arrange them in an organized manner on the baking sheet. Apply a thin layer of 2-3 tablespoons of olive oil onto the slices and lightly sprinkle them with a pinch of sea salt. Bake in the preheated oven until the crostini are golden and crisp.
4. Serve the artichoke and olive tapenade with the freshly baked crostini, garnished with the remaining chopped parsley and optional shredded Parmesan cheese.

Nutritional breakdown per serving:

Calories: 150 kcal, Protein: 3 grams, Carbohydrates: 14 grams, Fat: 10 grams, Saturated Fat: 1 grams, Cholesterol: 0 milligrams, Sodium: 350 milligrams, Fiber: 3 grams, and Sugar: 1 grams.

CUCUMBER AND YOGURT DIP WITH PITA BREAD

Total Cooking Time: 15 minutes
Prep Time: 10-15 minutes
Servings: 4-12 servings

Ingredients
For the Cucumber and Yogurt Dip:

- 1 1/2 cupsplainGreekyogurt
- Grate and drain 1 medium English or hothouse cucumber
- 2 smallgarliccloves, minced
- 2 tablespoonsextravirginoliveoil
- Scant 1/2 teaspoonsalt
- Optional: Chopped dill, lemon juice, and black pepper for seasoning

For the Pita Bread (if homemade):

- Breadflour
- Activedryyeast
- Salt
- Granulatedsugar
- Oliveoil

DetailedDirections
For the Cucumber and Yogurt Dip:

1. In a mixing bowl, combine the plain Greek yogurt, grated and squeezed cucumber, minced garlic, extra virgin olive oil, and salt.
2. Optionally, add chopped dill, a splash of lemon juice, and black pepper to season the dip to taste.
3. To ensure complete integration, be sure to stir all the ingredients together thoroughly. Place the mixture in the refrigerator for a minimum of 1 hour prior to serving, allowing it to cool and intensify the flavors.

<u>For the Pita Bread (if homemade):</u>

1. Follow the specific recipe for homemade pita bread, which typically involves preparing the dough, allowing it to rise, shaping the individual pitas, and baking them in the oven until they puff up and develop a golden color.

Nutritional breakdown per serving:

Calories: 150 kcal, Protein: 10 grams, Carbohydrates: 30 grams, Fat: 10 grams, Saturated Fat: 4 grams, Cholesterol: 10 milligrams, Sodium: 250 milligrams, Fiber: 4 grams, and Sugar: 2 grams.

STUFFED DATES

Total Cooking Time: 15 minutes
Prep Time: 8 minutes
Servings: 12 servings

Ingredients:

- 36 pitteddates
- 1 cup of your preferred nut butter
- 36 wholealmonds
- Optional: 1/4 cup shredded coconut for coating

Directions:

1. Carefully slice open each date and remove the pit, creating a small cavity in the center.
2. Fill each date with a small amount of nut butter, using a spoon or a piping bag for precision.
3. Press a whole almond into the center of each filled date, ensuring it is secure.
4. If desired, you can enhance the taste and texture by rolling the stuffed dates in shredded coconut.
5. Arrange the stuffed dates on a serving platter and chill in the refrigerator for at least 30 minutes prior to serving. This process allows the flavors to blend and combine harmoniously.

Nutritional breakdown per serving:

Calories: 68 kcal, Protein: 2 grams, Carbohydrates: 18 grams, Fat: 1 grams, Saturated Fat: 0 grams, Cholesterol: 0 milligrams, Sodium: 120 milligrams, Fiber: 2 grams, and Sugar: 4 grams.

HERBED FETA SPREAD

Total Cooking Time: 10 minutes
Prep Time: 10 minutes
Servings: 1 servings

Ingredients:

- 8 ouncesfetacheese
- 3/4 cup Greek yogurt
- 1 mediumclovegarlic, minced
- 1 tablespoon extra-virgin olive oil
- Koshersalt
- Freshly ground black pepper
- Fresh herbs such as dill, oregano, or thyme for additional flavor

Directions:

1. Place feta cheese, Greek yogurt, and minced garlic in a food processor or blender. Continue blending or processing the ingredients until they are thoroughly combined into a smooth mixture, making sure to scrape down the sides of the container as needed.
2. Blend the extra-virgin olive oil into the mixture until it is completely integrated.
3. If desired, pass the spread through a fine-mesh strainer for a silkier texture.
4. Add salt and pepper to the spread according to your taste preferences. If desired, you can also incorporate fresh herbs like dill, oregano, or thyme to enhance the flavor.
5. Utilize the herbed feta spread according to your preference, whether it is as a dip for vegetables, a spread for sandwiches, or a tasty complement to a variety of dishes.

Nutritional breakdown per serving:

Calories: 398 kcal, Protein: 32 grams, Carbohydrates: 12 grams, Fat: 8 grams, Saturated Fat: 1 grams, Cholesterol: 0 milligrams, Sodium: 100 milligrams, Fiber: 3 grams, and Sugar: 2 grams.

OLIVE OIL AND ZA'ATAR DIP

Total Cooking Time: 5-10 minutes
Prep Time: 5-10 minutes
Servings: 1 servings

Ingredients:

- 1/4 cupza'atarseasoningblend
- 1/2 cupextra-virginoliveoil
- Optional: Freshly squeezed lemon juice for added tang

Directions:

1. In a small bowl, combine the za'atar seasoning blend and extra-virgin olive oil.
2. Mix the ingredients thoroughly until the za'atar is evenly distributed throughout the olive oil.
3. To enhance the taste with a zesty and tangy twist, you can choose to include a small amount of freshly squeezed lemon juice if desired.
4. Present the olive oil and za'atar dip in a shallow dish or bowl, allowing it to be used as a delectable dip or as a flavorful drizzle for a variety of dishes.

Nutritional breakdown per serving:

Calories: 124 kcal, Protein: 1 grams, Carbohydrates: 1 grams, Fat: 14 grams, Saturated Fat: 4 grams, Cholesterol: 0 milligrams, Sodium: 20 milligrams, Fiber: 1 grams, and Sugar: 0 grams.

TOMATO AND OLIVE BRUSCHETTA

Total Cooking Time: 15 minutes
Prep Time: 15 minutes
Servings: 10 servings

Ingredients:

- 1 pound of plum tomatoes, roughly 4 to 5 large ones, or select another type of ripe tomatoes
- 1 teaspoonkoshersalt
- 5 tablespoonsextra-virginoliveoil
- 2 largegarliccloves, minced
- 8 largebasilleaves
- 1/4 cupza'atarseasoningblend
- 1/2 cuppittedandchoppedolives
- Grilled or toasted crusty bread, for serving

Directions:

1. Chop the tomatoes and place them in a colander. Shower them with salt and allow them to drain for at least 15 minutes to enhance their flavor.
2. In a bowl, combine the drained tomatoes, minced garlic, chopped olives, and za'atar seasoning blend.
3. Stir in the extra-virgin olive oil and gently fold in the basil leaves.
4. Grill or toast the crusty bread slices until they are golden and crisp.
5. Place the mixture of tomatoes and olives on the grilled or toasted bread slices before serving.

Nutritional breakdown per serving:

Calories: 180 kcal, Protein: 3 grams, Carbohydrates: 16 grams, Fat: 4 grams, Saturated Fat: 1 grams, Cholesterol: 57 milligrams, Sodium: 220 milligrams, Fiber: 1 grams, and Sugar: 2 grams.

CHAPTER 3
SOUPS AND
SALADS

CHICKPEA SALAD

Total Cooking Time: 15 minutes

Prep Time: 15 minutes

Servings: 5-6 servings

Ingredients:

- 1 tablespoon extra virgin olive oil
- Juiceof 1 lemon
- Zestof 1/2 lemon
- 1 teaspoonseasalt
- Blackpepper, totaste
- 4 cups cooked and unsalted chickpeas
- 1 pint of tomatoes, diced or halved
- 1 large cucumber, diced
- 1 redbellpepper, diced
- Optional: You may choose to enhance the flavor with fresh herbs like parsley or basil

Directions:

1. Combine the extra virgin olive oil (or tahini), lemon juice, lemon zest, sea salt, and black pepper in a large mixing bowl, ensuring they are well blended.
2. Add the cooked chickpeas, diced tomatoes, diced cucumber, and diced red bell pepper to the bowl.
3. Carefully mix the ingredients until they are thoroughly coated with the dressing.
4. If desired, add fresh herbs such as parsley or basil for an additional layer of flavor.
5. Serve the Mediterranean chickpea salad immediately, or refrigerate it for a few hours to allow the flavors to meld before serving

Nutritional breakdown per serving: Calories:

150 kcal, Protein: 8 grams, Carbohydrates: 25 grams, Fat: 8 grams, Saturated Fat: 1 grams, Cholesterol: 0 milligrams, Sodium: 200 milligrams, Fiber: 6 grams, and Sugar: 2 grams.

MINTY CUCUMBER YOGURT DIP

Total Cooking Time: 10-15 minutes
Prep Time: 10-15 minutes
Servings: 1 serving

Ingredients:

- 1 cupGreekyogurt
- 1/2 cucumber, finelydicedorgrated
- 2-3 tablespoonsfreshmint, finelychopped
- 1-2 clovesgarlic, minced
- 1 tablespoonextravirginoliveoil
- 1 tablespoonlemonjuice
- Saltandpeppertotaste
- Optional: Cayenne pepper for a hint of spice

Directions:

1. In a mixing bowl, blend together Greek yogurt, cucumber (finely diced or grated), fresh mint (finely chopped), minced garlic, extra virgin olive oil, and lemon juice until thoroughly combined.
2. Add a pinch of salt, pepper, and, if desired, a hint of cayenne pepper to the mixture to elevate its spiciness.
3. Stir the ingredients until well combined, ensuring the flavors are evenly distributed.
4. Sample the meal and modify the seasoning based on your personal taste, incorporating additional salt, pepper, or lemon juice as necessary.
5. Before serving, refrigerate the minty cucumber yogurt dip for a minimum of 30 minutes to let the flavors blend together.

Nutritional breakdown per serving:

Calories: 70 kcal, Protein: 5 grams, Carbohydrates: 8 grams, Fat: 4 grams, Saturated Fat: 1 grams, Cholesterol: 5 milligrams, Sodium: 200 milligrams, Fiber: 2 grams, and Sugar: 4 grams.

GREEK FETA AND OLIVE TAPENADE

Total Cooking Time: 10-15 minutes
Prep Time: 10-15 minutes
Servings: 1 serving

Ingredients:

- 1 cuppittedKalamataolives
- 1/2 cuppittedCastelvetranoolives
- 1/4 cupcrumbledfetacheese
- 2 tablespoonschoppedfreshparsley
- 2 tablespoonscapers
- 2 tablespoonslemonjuice
- 2 tablespoonsextravirginoliveoil
- 2 clovesgarlic, minced

Directions:

1. In a food processor, mix the pitted Kalamata olives, pitted Castelvetrano olives, crumbled feta cheese, chopped fresh parsley, capers, minced garlic, lemon juice, and extra virgin olive oil until they are thoroughly combined.
2. Pulse the ingredients until they are coarsely chopped and well combined, ensuring that the tapenade retains texture and is not overprocessed into a paste.
3. Taste the tapenade and adjust the seasoning if necessary, adding more lemon juice or olive oil as desired.
4. Place the Greek feta and olive tapenade into a serving bowl, and if desired, you can add a delicate drizzle of extra virgin olive oil as a finishing touch.
5. Serve the tapenade with crackers, crostini, or crusty bread, or use it as a flavorful spread for sandwiches and wraps.

Nutritional breakdown per serving:

Calories: 90 kcal, Protein: 3 grams, Carbohydrates: 4 grams, Fat: 8 grams, Saturated Fat: 3 grams, Cholesterol: 15 milligrams, Sodium: 300 milligrams, Fiber: 2 grams, and Sugar: 0 grams.

TUNA SALAD

Total Cooking Time: 10-15 minutes
Prep Time: 10-15 minutes
Servings: 1 serving

Ingredients:

- 2 (5-oz.) cans white tuna, packed in water
- 1/2 cupmayonnaise
- 2 tablespoonsfinelychoppedfreshdill
- 1 teaspoonkoshersalt
- 1/2 teaspoonfreshlygroundblackpepper
- 2 tablespoonsfreshlemonjuice, divided
- 1/2 cupfinelychoppeddillpickles
- Additional ingredients based on other sources: Dijon mustard, lime zest, lime juice, extra virgin olive oil, sumac, red pepper flakes, celery, cucumber, radish, green onions, red onion, mint, parsley, pitted Kalamata olives, capers

Directions:

1. Combine the canned tuna, mayonnaise, finely chopped fresh dill, kosher salt, freshly ground black pepper, and 1 tablespoon of fresh lemon juice in a medium-sized bowl, stirring until the ingredients are thoroughly mixed. Mix the ingredients together well to ensure they are evenly combined.
2. Add the finely chopped dill pickles to the tuna mixture and gently fold them in until evenly distributed.
3. In a small separate bowl, whisk together Dijon mustard, lime zest, lime juice, extra virgin olive oil, sumac, and red pepper flakes to make the no-mayo salad dressing. Customize the seasoning by adding kosher salt and pepper to your liking.
4. In a spacious mixing bowl, mix together the chopped vegetables (celery, cucumber, radish, green onions, and red onion), along with the chopped mint and parsley, and pitted Kalamata olives (or capers).
5. Drizzle the zesty Dijon dressing over the tuna salad ingredients and thoroughly combine. Place a cover over the mixture and refrigerate it for around 30 minutes. Before serving, gently mix the salad once more to redistribute the dressing.

Nutritional breakdown per serving:

Calories: 300 kcal, Protein: 25 grams, Carbohydrates: 8 grams, Fat: 10 grams, Saturated Fat: 3 grams, Cholesterol: 35 milligrams, Sodium: 500 milligrams, Fiber: 4 grams, and Sugar: 2 grams.

ZESTY LEMON-HERB MARINATED OLIVES

Total Cooking Time: 10 minutes
Prep Time: 5 minutes
Servings: 1 serving

Ingredients:

- 2 cups mixed olives (such as Kalamata, green, and black olives)
- 2 tablespoons extra-virgin olive oil
- Zest of 1 lemon
- Juice of 1 lemon
- 2 cloves garlic, minced
- 1 tablespoon fresh parsley, chopped
- 1 tablespoon fresh thyme leaves
- 1 teaspoon red pepper flakes
- Salt and pepper to taste

Directions:

1. In a mixing bowl, combine the olives, extra-virgin olive oil, lemon zest, lemon juice, minced garlic, chopped parsley, thyme leaves, red pepper flakes, salt, and pepper.
2. Toss the olives gently to ensure they are coated evenly with the marinade.
3. Allow the olives to marinate for at least 30 minutes to let the flavors meld together. For a more intense flavor, marinate them for up to 24 hours in the refrigerator.
4. Before serving, give the olives a quick toss to redistribute the marinade.
5. Serve the Zesty Lemon-Herb Marinated Olives as a flavorful appetizer or as part of a cheese or charcuterie board.

Nutritional breakdown per serving:

Calories: 80 kcal, Protein: 1 grams, Carbohydrates: 4 grams, Fat: 2 grams, Saturated Fat: 1 grams, Cholesterol: 0 milligrams, Sodium: 400 milligrams, Fiber: 2 grams, and Sugar: 0 grams.

TOMATO AND CUCUMBER SOUP

Total Cooking Time: 15-20 minutes
Prep Time: 10 to 15 minutes
Servings: 4 servings

Ingredients:

- 1 long European cucumber or 4 Persian cucumbers, peeled and roughly chopped
- Quarter 1 1/2 pounds of ripe tomatoes
- 2 rinsedonionslices
- 2 large garlic cloves, halved and with the green germs removed
- 2 tablespoonssherryvinegar
- 2 tablespoonsextravirginoliveoil
- Salttotaste
- Slivered fresh basil leaves or very small whole basil leaves for garnish

Directions:

1. Combine chopped cucumbers, quartered tomatoes, onion slices, halved garlic cloves, sherry vinegar, and extra virgin olive oil in a blender or food processor. Continue blending the ingredients until they are fully incorporated and the mixture becomes smooth and cohesive.
2. Puree the blend until it reaches a smooth consistency, then add salt according to your personal preference.
3. Pour the soup into a spacious bowl, cover it, and place it in the refrigerator for a minimum of 2 hours to ensure it is thoroughly chilled.
4. Before serving, garnish the soup with slivered fresh basil leaves or very small whole basil leaves.

Nutritional breakdown per serving:

Calories: 120 kcal, Protein: 4 grams, Carbohydrates: 18 grams, Fat: 4 grams, Saturated Fat: 1 grams, Cholesterol: 0 milligrams, Sodium: 350 milligrams, Fiber: 4 grams, and Sugar: 8 grams.

FETA AND WATERMELON SALAD

The total cooking: 5 minutes

Time prep: 5 minutes

Serving: 1

Ingredients:

- 2 pounds seedless watermelon, thinly sliced into large, irregular pieces
- 2 tablespoons white or red balsamic vinegar
- Salt
- 1 (6-ounce) block Greek feta, thinly sliced into large, irregular pieces
- 3 tablespoonsextra-virginoliveoil
- Freshlygroundblackpepper
- Leaves from 1 sprig basil, larger leaves torn

DetailedDirections

1. Thinly slice the seedless watermelon into large, irregular pieces.
2. Place the watermelon slices in an attractive arrangement on a serving platter.
3. Drizzle the watermelon with white or red balsamic vinegar and sprinkle with salt.
4. Arrange the thinly sliced Greek feta over the watermelon.
5. Gently pour a drizzle of extra-virgin olive oil over the salad and add a sprinkle of freshly ground black pepper to season.
6. Add torn basil leaves as a garnish on top.

Nutritional breakdown per serving:

Calories: 200 kcal, Protein: 7 grams, Carbohydrates: 28 grams, Fat: 12 grams, Saturated Fat: 5 grams, Cholesterol: 30 milligrams, Sodium: 300 milligrams, Fiber: 2 grams, and Sugar: 10 grams.

LEMON CHICKEN SALAD

Total Cooking Time: 10-15 minutes
Prep Time: 10 minutes
Servings: 4-6 servings

Ingredients:

- 2 boneless, skinlesschickenbreasts
- 1 tablespoonoliveoil
- Saltandpeppertotaste
- 4 cupsmixedsaladgreens
- 1 cupcherrytomatoes, halved
- 1/2 cupslicedcucumber
- 1/4 cupslicedredonion
- 1/4 cupslicedblackolives
- 1/4 cupcrumbledfetacheese
- 2 tablespoonsfreshlemonjuice
- 2 tablespoonsextra-virginoliveoil
- 1 teaspoonDijonmustard
- 1 clovegarlic, minced
- 1 teaspoondriedoregano

Directions:

1. Firstly, set the oven temperature to 400°F (200°C). Following that, generously season both sides of the chicken breasts with salt and pepper.
2. To start, heat the olive oil in an oven-safe skillet over medium-high heat. Then, carefully place the chicken breasts in the skillet and cook them for about 2-3 minutes on each side until they are beautifully browned.
3. Once you have achieved a nice brown color on the chicken by browning it on the stovetop, gently move the skillet to the preheated oven. Allow the chicken to roast for approximately 5-10 minutes, or until it is fully cooked. Remove from the oven and let it rest for a few minutes. Then, slice the chicken into thin strips.
4. To create a delicious salad, gather a generous amount of mixed salad greens, cherry tomatoes, sliced cucumber, red onion, black olives, and crumbled feta cheese in a

large salad bowl. Combine these ingredients together for a delightful medley of flavors.

5. To prepare a delectable dressing, take a small bowl and combine the fresh lemon juice, extra-virgin olive oil, Dijon mustard, minced garlic, dried oregano, salt, and pepper. Whisk these ingredients together until they are well blended and create a flavorful dressing.

6. Carefully drizzle the dressing over the salad ingredients in the bowl, ensuring it is evenly distributed. Toss the salad ingredients together carefully, ensuring that each component is coated with the dressing.

7. Add the sliced chicken to the salad and gently toss to combine all the ingredients.

8. Take a moment to taste the salad and, if desired, make adjustments to the seasoning by adding salt, pepper, or a touch more lemon juice to suit your preferences.

9. Serve the Lemon Chicken Salad as a light and refreshing main course or as a side dish.

Nutritional breakdown per serving:

Calories: 280 kcal, Protein: 25 grams, Carbohydrates: 15 grams, Fat: 15 grams, Saturated Fat: 3 grams, Cholesterol: 100 milligrams, Sodium: 500 milligrams, Fiber: 4 grams, and Sugar: 4 grams.

QUINOA TABBOULEH SALAD

Total Cooking Time: 15 minutes
Prep Time: 10 minutes
Servings: 4-6 servings

Ingredients:

- 1/2 cup of uncooked quinoa
- 3 cups chopped parsley
- 1/4 cup of chopped mint
- 1/3 cup of cubed cherry tomatoes
- 1/3 cup chopped red onion
- 3 tbsp lemon juice1/4 cup olive oil
- 2 tspdijonmustard
- 1 garlicclove, finelychopped
- 1 tspmaplesyrup
- Saltandpepper

DetailedDirections

1. To start, rinse the quinoa with cold water and cook it following the instructions on the package. After cooking, let it cool.
2. In a spacious bowl, mix together the cooked and cooled quinoa, chopped parsley, chopped mint, cubed cherry tomatoes, and chopped red onion.
3. In a different bowl, combine the lemon juice, olive oil, Dijon mustard, finely chopped garlic, maple syrup, salt, and pepper. Whisk them together to create the dressing.
4. Drizzle the dressing over the mixture of quinoa and herbs, and toss everything together until thoroughly combined.

Nutritional breakdown per serving:

Calories: 250 kcal, Protein: 8 grams, Carbohydrates: 30 grams, Fat: 8 grams, Saturated Fat: 2 grams, Cholesterol: 0 milligrams, Sodium: 300 milligrams, Fiber: 6 grams, and Sugar: 4 grams.

ROASTED RED PEPPER HUMMUS

Total Cooking Time: 15 minutes
Prep Time: 10 minutes
Servings: 4-6 servings

Ingredients:

- 1 can chickpeas, rinsed and drained
- 2 roasted red peppers, peeled and seeded
- 2 clovesgarlic, minced
- 3 tablespoonstahini
- 3 tablespoonsfreshlemonjuice
- 2 tablespoonsextra-virginoliveoil
- 1/2 teaspoongroundcumin
- Saltandpeppertotaste
- Optional garnish: drizzle of olive oil, sprinkle of paprika, and chopped fresh parsley

Directions:

1. Add the chickpeas, roasted red peppers, minced garlic, tahini, fresh lemon juice, extra-virgin olive oil, ground cumin, salt, and pepper to a food processor or blender. Combine the ingredients by mixing or blending them until they are well incorporated. Continue blending the mixture until it becomes smooth and thoroughly blended.

2. Continue blending the ingredients until they achieve a smooth and creamy texture, ensuring to scrape down the sides of the bowl as needed to ensure even blending. In case the mixture is too thick, you have the option to add a small amount of water or additional olive oil to attain the desired consistency.

3. Take a moment to taste the hummus and make any necessary adjustments to the seasoning by adding salt, pepper, and lemon juice as desired. If you prefer a more pronounced flavor, feel free to incorporate additional roasted red peppers.

4. Once the hummus is smooth and well seasoned, transfer it to a serving bowl.

5. For garnish, drizzle a little olive oil over the top of the hummus. Enhance the visual appeal by sprinkling paprika over the hummus, adding a vibrant burst of color. To add an additional element of freshness, consider adorning the dish with finely chopped fresh parsley.

6. Present the Roasted Red Pepper Hummus alongside pita bread, a variety of fresh vegetables, or use it as a delectable spread for sandwiches and wraps.

Nutritional breakdown per serving:

Calories: 100 kcal, Protein: 3 grams, Carbohydrates: 8 grams, Fat: 5 grams, Saturated Fat: 1 grams, Cholesterol: 0 milligrams, Sodium: 200 milligrams, Fiber: 4 grams, and Sugar: 2 grams.

MEDITERRANEAN CHICKPEA AND SPINACH SALAD

Total Cooking Time: 15 minutes
Prep Time: 10 minutes
Servings: 4-6 servings

Ingredients:

- 2 cups canned chickpeas, rinsed and drained
- 4 cupsfreshspinachleaves
- 1 cupcherrytomatoes, halved
- 1/2 cupcucumber, diced
- 1/4 cupredonion, thinlysliced
- 1/4 cup of pitted and halved Kalamata olives
- 1/4 cupcrumbledfetacheese
- 2 tablespoonsfreshlemonjuice
- 2 tablespoonsextra-virginoliveoil
- 1 teaspoondriedoregano
- Saltandpeppertotaste

Directions:

1. In a spacious mixing bowl, mix together the chickpeas, spinach leaves, cherry tomatoes, cucumber, red onion, Kalamata olives, and crumbled feta cheese.
2. To prepare the dressing, combine fresh lemon juice, extra-virgin olive oil, dried oregano, salt, and pepper in a small bowl. Whisk the ingredients together until well blended.
3. Evenly distribute the dressing over the salad ingredients in the large bowl, ensuring that all components are coated. Thoroughly toss the salad to ensure an even distribution of the dressing, ensuring that each ingredient is well coated.
4. Sample the salad and make any necessary adjustments to the seasoning by adding salt and pepper to taste. If desired, you can also add more lemon juice or olive oil based on your personal preference.
5. Let the salad rest for a few minutes to allow the flavors to blend together.

6. Enjoy the Mediterranean Chickpea and Spinach Salad as a delightful and revitalizing main course or as a complementary side dish to accompany grilled chicken or fish.

Nutritional breakdown per serving:

Calories: 300 kcal, Protein: 10 grams, Carbohydrates: 32 grams, Fat: 12 grams, Saturated Fat: 1 grams, Cholesterol: 0 milligrams, Sodium: 400 milligrams, Fiber: 10 grams, and Sugar: 4 grams.

CUCUMBER AND DILL SOUP

Total Cooking Time: 15 minutes
Prep Time: 10 minutes
Servings: 4-6 servings

Ingredients:

- 2 largecucumbers, peeledanddiced
- 1 cupplainGreekyogurt
- 1/2 cupfreshdill, chopped
- 1/4 cupfreshmintleaves, chopped
- 1 clovegarlic, minced
- 1 tablespoonlemonjuice
- 1 tablespoonextra-virginoliveoil
- Saltandpeppertotaste
- Optional garnish: croutons, chopped cucumber, and dill sprigs

Directions:

1. Combine the diced cucumbers, Greek yogurt, fresh dill, mint leaves, minced garlic, lemon juice, and extra-virgin olive oil in a blender or food processor. Continue blending the mixture until it becomes smooth and creamy in texture.
2. Sample the mixture and season it with salt and pepper to your liking. Modify the flavors as necessary by incorporating additional lemon juice or dill.
3. Once you have blended the soup, transfer it to a large bowl and place it in the refrigerator for a minimum of 1 hour. This will help chill the soup and allow the flavors to blend together harmoniously.
4. Once chilled, give the soup a stir and taste again for any necessary seasoning adjustments.
5. Ladle the cucumber and dill soup into individual serving bowls. If desired, garnish with croutons, chopped cucumber, and dill sprigs for added texture and presentation.
6. Serve the soup immediately and enjoy its refreshing flavors.

Nutritional breakdown per serving: Calories:

100 kcal, Protein: 3 grams, Carbohydrates: 7 grams, Fat: 7 grams, Saturated Fat: 2 grams, Cholesterol: 0 milligrams, Sodium: 250 milligrams, Fiber: 2 grams, and Sugar: 5 grams.

MILLET SALAD

Total Cooking Time: 15 minutes
Prep Time: 10 minutes
Servings: 4 servings

Ingredients:

- 1 cupcookedmillet
- 1 cupcherrytomatoes, halved
- 1 cucumber, diced
- 1 redbellpepper, diced
- 1/4 cupredonion, finelychopped
- 1/4 cupfreshparsley, chopped
- 1/4 cupfetacheese, crumbled
- 1/4 cup of pitted and halved Kalamata olives

Forthedressing:

- 2 tablespoonsoliveoil
- 1 tablespoonlemonjuice
- 1 clovegarlic, minced
- Saltandpeppertotaste

Directions:

1. Add the cooked millet, cherry tomatoes, cucumber, red bell pepper, red onion, parsley, feta cheese, and Kalamata olives to a large mixing bowl. Delicately toss and blend all of the ingredients until they are evenly combined. Make sure to thoroughly mix the mixture to ensure a well-blended result.
2. In a small bowl, mix together the olive oil, lemon juice, minced garlic, salt, and pepper until well combined. Use a whisk to blend the ingredients and create a flavorful dressing.
3. Evenly distribute the dressing over the millet salad and toss it well to make sure all the ingredients are coated.
4. Pause for a moment to sample the salad and, if needed, sprinkle a small amount of salt and pepper to fine-tune the seasoning.

5. Sprinkle the salad with almonds or any other desired toppings for added crunch and flavor.
6. After ensuring that all the ingredients are thoroughly combined, either transfer the millet salad to a serving dish or serve it without delay.

Nutritional breakdown per serving:

Calories: 250 kcal, Protein: 8 grams, Carbohydrates: 35 grams, Fat: 8 grams, Saturated Fat: 0 grams, Cholesterol: 0 milligrams, Sodium: 10 milligrams, Fiber: 6 grams, and Sugar: 0 grams.

CHICKPEA AND CUCUMBER SALAD

Total Cooking Time: 10-15 minutes

Prep Time: 10 minutes

Servings: 4 servings

Ingredients:

- 2 (15-ounce cans) chickpeas, drained and rinsed
- 1 largecucumber, diced
- 1 redbellpepper, diced
- 2 cupscherrytomatoes, halved
- ½ cupredonion, diced
- 4 ouncesfetacheese, crumbled
- ½ cupfinelychoppedparsley
- Lemonvinaigrette

DetailedDirections

1. Add the chickpeas, diced cucumber, diced red bell pepper, halved cherry tomatoes, diced red onion, crumbled feta cheese, and finely chopped parsley to a large mixing bowl. Blend all the ingredients together until they are fully incorporated.
2. Prepare the lemon vinaigrette and pour it over the salad ingredients.
3. Gently combine all the ingredients until they are fully coated with the dressing. Serve the Mediterranean Chickpea and Cucumber Salad promptly.

Nutritional breakdown per serving:

Calories: 250 kcal, Protein: 10 grams, Carbohydrates: 25 grams, Fat: 10 grams, Saturated Fat: 2 grams, Cholesterol: 0 milligrams, Sodium: 400 milligrams, Fiber: 6 grams, and Sugar: 4 grams.

ORZO SALAD WITH SUN-DRIED TOMATOES

Total Cooking Time: 15 minutes
Prep Time: 10 minutes
Servings: 4 servings

Ingredients:

- 1 cuporzopasta
- 1/2 cupsun-driedtomatoes, chopped
- 1/4 cup Kalamata olives, pitted and halved
- 1/4 cupcrumbledfetacheese
- 1/4 cupfreshparsley, chopped
- 2 tablespoonsextravirginoliveoil
- 2 tablespoonslemonjuice
- 1 clovegarlic, minced
- Saltandpeppertotaste

Directions:

4. Prepare the orzo pasta as per the instructions on the package. Once cooked, drain the pasta and allow it to cool. Set it aside for later use.
5. In a spacious bowl, mix together the cooked orzo, sun-dried tomatoes, pitted Kalamata olives, feta cheese, and freshly chopped parsley.
6. In a small bowl, mix together the extra virgin olive oil, lemon juice, minced garlic, salt, and pepper. Utilize a whisk to completely incorporate and blend all of the ingredients together.
7. Drizzle the dressing onto the orzo salad and delicately toss until thoroughly mixed.
8. Before serving, give the salad a gentle toss and adjust the seasoning if needed.

Nutritional breakdown per serving:

Calories: 300 kcal, Protein: 10 grams, Carbohydrates: 36 grams, Fat: 8 grams, Saturated Fat: 1 grams, Cholesterol: 5 milligrams, Sodium: 400 milligrams, Fiber: 5 grams, and Sugar: 4 grams.

QUINOA TUNA SALAD

Total Cooking Time: 15 minutes
Prep Time: 10 minutes
Servings: 4-6 servings

Ingredients:

- 1 cupquinoa
- 2 cupswater
- 1 can (5 oz) tuna, drained
- 1 cupcherrytomatoes, halved
- 1/2 cupcucumber, diced
- 1/4 cupredonion, finelychopped
- 1/4 cup sliced pitted Kalamata olives
- 1/4 cupfreshparsley, chopped
- 1/4 cupfetacheese, crumbled
- 3 tablespoonsextravirginoliveoil
- 2 tablespoonslemonjuice
- Saltandpeppertotaste

DetailedDirections

1. To prepare the quinoa, rinse it under cold water. Then, in a medium saucepan, bring water to a boil and add the quinoa. Reduce the heat, cover the saucepan, and let it simmer for about 15 minutes or until the quinoa is tender and the water is fully absorbed.
2. In a spacious bowl, mix together the cooked quinoa, drained tuna, cherry tomatoes, cucumber, red onion, Kalamata olives, and fresh parsley.
3. In a compact bowl, combine the extra virgin olive oil and lemon juice by whisking them together. Drizzle the dressing over the mixture of quinoa and tuna, then toss everything together to ensure it is well combined.
4. Gently fold in the crumbled feta cheese.
5. Adjust the amount of salt and pepper to suit your personal taste.
6. Serve the Mediterranean Quinoa Tuna Salad as a light and protein-rich meal or a refreshing side dish.

Nutritional breakdown per serving:

Calories: 350 kcal, Protein: 25 grams, Carbohydrates: 35 grams, Fat: 15 grams, Saturated Fat: 3 grams, Cholesterol: 30 milligrams, Sodium: 450 milligrams, Fiber: 6 grams, and Sugar: 4 grams.

LEMON CHICKPEA AND SPINACH SALAD

Total Cooking Time: 15 minutes
Prep Time: 10 minutes
Servings: 4-6 servings

Ingredients:

- 2 (15-ounce cans) chickpeas, drained and rinsed
- 1 largecucumber, diced
- 1 redbellpepper, diced
- 2 cupscherrytomatoes, halved
- 1/2 cupredonion, diced
- 4 ouncesfetacheese, crumbled
- 1/2 cupfinelychoppedparsley
- Lemon vinaigrette (use as much or as little as desired)

DetailedDirections

1. In a large mixing bowl, combine the chickpeas, diced cucumber, diced red bell pepper, halved cherry tomatoes, diced red onion, crumbled feta cheese, and finely chopped parsley.
2. Drizzle the desired quantity of lemon vinaigrette over the salad and delicately mix until thoroughly incorporated.
3. Serve the Mediterranean Lemon Chickpea and Spinach Salad immediately as a refreshing and nutritious dish.

Nutritional breakdown per serving:

Calories: 250 kcal, Protein: 10 grams, Carbohydrates: 25 grams, Fat: 10 grams, Saturated Fat: 2 grams, Cholesterol: 0 milligrams, Sodium: 400 milligrams, Fiber: 8 grams, and Sugar: 4 grams.

TOMATO AND MOZZARELLA SKEWERS

Total Cooking Time: 10 minutes
Prep Time: 10 minutes
Servings: 16 skewers

Ingredients:

- 16 smallfreshmozzarellaballs
- 16 freshbasilleaves
- 16 cherrytomatoes
- Extra-virgin olive oil, to drizzle
- Coarse salt & freshly ground pepper, to taste

Directions:

1. Thread one mozzarella ball, one basil leaf, and one cherry tomato onto each small skewer.
2. Drizzle the assembled skewers with extra-virgin olive oil.
3. Add a desired amount of coarse salt and freshly ground pepper for seasoning.

Nutritional breakdown per serving:

Calories: 200 kcal, Protein: 12 grams, Carbohydrates: 6 grams, Fat: 12 grams, Saturated Fat: 5 grams, Cholesterol: 30 milligrams, Sodium: 300 milligrams, Fiber: 2 grams, and Sugar: 3 grams.

FETA AND HERB SPREAD

Total Cooking Time: 5 minutes
Prep Time: 5 minutes
Servings: 8 servings

Ingredients:

- 8 ouncesblockqualityfeta, drained
- 1/4 cupGreekyogurt
- Zestof 1 lemon
- 2 tablespoonsextravirginoliveoil

Directions:

1. Using a food processor, combine the feta cheese, Greek yogurt, lemon zest, and extra virgin olive oil until they are well blended.
2. Combine the ingredients and blend until a smooth and creamy consistency is reached, adjusting the quantity of olive oil as needed to achieve the desired texture.
3. Sample the dish and fine-tune the seasoning, incorporating additional lemon zest or olive oil if needed.
4. Transfer the spread to a serving bowl.

Nutritional breakdown per serving:

Calories: 150 kcal, Protein: 7 grams, Carbohydrates: 4 grams, Fat: 10 grams, Saturated Fat: 7 grams, Cholesterol: 30 milligrams, Sodium: 300 milligrams, Fiber: 0 grams, and Sugar: 2 grams.

SPICED ALMONDS

Total Cooking Time: 15 minutes
Prep Time: 10 minutes
Servings: 8 servings

Ingredients:

- 2 cups whole almonds
- 1 tablespoon olive oil
- 1 teaspoon ground cumin
- 1 teaspoon ground coriander
- 1 teaspoon smoked paprika
- 1/2 teaspoon ground cinnamon
- 1/4 teaspoon cayenne pepper
- 1 tablespoon brown sugar
- 1 teaspoon sea salt

Directions:

1. To start, set the oven temperature to 350°F (175°C) and wait for it to reach the desired preheating temperature.
2. In a bowl, ensure the almonds are thoroughly coated with olive oil by tossing them together until evenly distributed.
3. In a different bowl, combine the ground cumin, ground coriander, smoked paprika, ground cinnamon, cayenne pepper, brown sugar, and sea salt together.
4. Incorporate the spice mixture into the almonds and thoroughly toss until the almonds are evenly coated with the spices.
5. Lay out the almonds in a single, even layer on a baking sheet that has been lined with parchment paper.
6. Put the baking sheet with the almonds into the preheated oven and let them bake for around 10 to 12 minutes, or until they emit a delightful aroma and turn a slightly golden, toasted shade.
7. Allow the spiced almonds to cool before serving

Nutritional breakdown per serving:

Calories: 200 kcal, Protein: 7 grams, Carbohydrates: 7 grams, Fat: 12 grams, Saturated Fat: 2 grams, Cholesterol: 0 milligrams, Sodium: 200 milligrams, Fiber: 4 grams, and Sugar: 2 grams.

CHAPTER 4
SNACK RECIPES

LEMON GARLIC BUTTER GRILLED SCALLOPS

Total Cooking Time: 10-15 minutes
Prep Time: 10 minutes
Servings: 4 servings

Ingredients:

- 1 poundscallops
- 2 tablespoonsbutter, melted
- 2 tablespoonsoliveoil
- Juiceof 1 lemon
- 3 clovesgarlic, minced
- Saltandpepper, totaste
- Fresh parsley, chopped (for garnish)

DetailedDirections:

1. Preheat the grill to medium-high heat.
2. Take a small bowl and blend together the melted butter, olive oil, lemon juice, minced garlic, salt, and pepper.
3. Gently remove any moisture from the scallops using a paper towel, and then transfer them to a shallow dish.
4. Drizzle the lemon garlic butter mixture over the scallops, ensuring they are thoroughly coated. Allow the scallops to marinate for approximately 5 minutes.
5. Position the scallops on the preheated grill and grill each side for approximately 2-3 minutes until they turn opaque and thoroughly cooked. Be cautious not to overcook them to avoid toughness.
6. Take the scallops off the grill and allow them to rest for a few minutes.
7. Garnish with fresh chopped parsley.
8. Serve the grilled scallops with lemon garlic butter as a hot main dish or appetizer option.

Nutritional breakdown per serving:

Calories: 200 kcal, Protein: 20 grams, Carbohydrates: 4 grams, Fat: 12 grams, Saturated Fat: 4 grams, Cholesterol: 45 milligrams, Sodium: 400 milligrams, Fiber: 0 grams, and Sugar: 0 grams.

LEMON HERB GRILLED SHRIMP WRAPS

Total Cooking Time: 10-15 minutes
Prep Time: 10 minutes
Servings: 4 servings

Ingredients:

- 1 poundshrimp, peeledanddeveined
- 2 tablespoonsoliveoil
- Juiceof 1 lemon
- 2 clovesgarlic, minced
- 1 teaspoondriedoregano
- Saltandpepper, totaste
- 4 largetortillawraps
- Lettuceleaves
- Slicedtomatoes
- Slicedcucumbers
- Slicedredonions
- Tzatziki sauce or your favorite dressing (optional)

DetailedDirections:

1. Preheat the grill to medium-high heat.
2. Place the shrimp in a mixing bowl and add olive oil, lemon juice, minced garlic, dried oregano, salt, and pepper. Mix well to ensure the shrimp is evenly coated.
3. As an option, you can decide to put the shrimp on skewers to avoid them from sliding through the grill grates.
4. Place the shrimp onto the preheated grill and cook for around 2 to 3 minutes per side, or until they become pink and are completely cooked.
5. Take the shrimp off the grill and allow them to cool down for a moment.
6. Warm the tortilla wraps according to package instructions.
7. Assemble the wraps by placing lettuce leaves, sliced tomatoes, cucumbers, and red onions on each tortilla.
8. Add the grilled shrimp on top of the vegetables.
9. Drizzle with tzatziki sauce or your favorite dressing, if desired.

10. Roll up the wraps tightly, tucking in the sides as you go.
11. Cut the wraps in half diagonally and serve.

Nutritional breakdown per serving:

Calories: 300 kcal, Protein: 28 grams, Carbohydrates: 220 grams, Fat: 10 grams, Saturated Fat: 2 grams, Cholesterol: 220 milligrams, Sodium: 600 milligrams, Fiber: 4 grams, and Sugar: 3 grams.

SHRIMP AND COUSCOUS SALAD

Total Cooking Time: 15 minutes
Prep Time: 10 minutes
Servings: 4 servings

Ingredients:

- 1 poundshrimp, peeledanddeveined
- 1 cupcouscous
- 1 1/4 cupswater
- 2 tablespoonsoliveoil
- 2 tablespoonslemonjuice
- 2 clovesgarlic, minced
- 1 teaspoondriedoregano
- Saltandpepper, totaste
- 1 cupcherrytomatoes, halved
- 1/2 cupcucumber, diced
- 1/4 cupredonion, thinlysliced
- 1/4 cup of pitted and halved Kalamata olives.
- 1/4 cupcrumbledfetacheese
- Fresh parsley, chopped (for garnish)

DetailedDirections:

1. Heat water in a medium-sized saucepan until it reaches a boiling point. Add couscous to the pan, cover, and remove from heat. Allow it to sit for 5 minutes, then fluff the couscous with a fork.
2. Add shrimp, olive oil, lemon juice, minced garlic, dried oregano, salt, and pepper to a mixing bowl. Stir the ingredients well to ensure they are completely combined. Next, gently toss the mixture together to evenly coat the shrimp.
3. To prepare for cooking, heat a skillet over medium-high heat and carefully add the shrimp to the hot skillet. Cook the shrimp for about 2-3 minutes on each side, or until they turn pink and are thoroughly cooked. After cooking, take the skillet off the heat source.

4. In a generously sized salad bowl, mix together the cooked couscous, cherry tomatoes, cucumber, red onion, Kalamata olives, and crumbled feta cheese.
5. Gently add the cooked shrimp to the salad bowl and carefully toss to combine all the ingredients together.
6. Enhance the dish with a sprinkling of freshly chopped parsley to bring a burst of freshness and flavor.
7. Serve the Mediterranean shrimp and couscous salad immediately.

Nutritional breakdown per serving:

Calories: 350 kcal, Protein: 26 grams, Carbohydrates: 35 grams, Fat: 12 grams, Saturated Fat: 3 grams, Cholesterol: 220 milligrams, Sodium: 500 milligrams, Fiber: 4 grams, and Sugar: 3 grams.

GREEK-STYLE GRILLED SEA BASS

Total Cooking Time: 8-10 minutes
Prep Time: 10 minutes
Servings: 4 servings

Ingredients:

- 4 seabassfillets
- 2 tablespoonsoliveoil
- Juiceof 1 lemon
- 2 clovesgarlic, minced
- 1 teaspoondriedoregano
- Saltandpepper, totaste
- Lemonwedges (forserving)

DetailedDirections:

1. Preheat the grill to medium-high heat.
2. Mix the olive oil, lemon juice, minced garlic, dried oregano, salt, and pepper together in a small bowl. Use a whisk to vigorously blend the ingredients until they are well combined.
3. Using the marinade mixture, coat both sides of the sea bass fillets by brushing them.
4. Arrange the sea bass fillets on the grill that has been preheated and cook for approximately 4-5 minutes per side. Verify that the fish is thoroughly cooked and easily flakes apart when probed with a fork. Remember that the cooking duration may vary depending on the thickness of the fillets.
5. Remove the sea bass from the grill and let it rest for a few minutes before serving.
6. Present the Greek-style grilled sea bass while it is hot, and provide lemon wedges on the side for those who wish to squeeze them over the fish.

Nutritional breakdown per serving:

Calories: 416 kcal, Protein: 54 grams, Carbohydrates: 4 grams, Fat: 20 grams, Saturated Fat: 8 grams, Cholesterol: 143 milligrams, Sodium: 400 milligrams, Fiber: 1 grams, and Sugar: 2 grams.

SHRIMP SKEWERS WITH TZATZIKI SAUCE

Total Cooking Time: 15 minutes
Prep Time: 10 minutes
Servings: 4 servings

Ingredients:

- 1 poundshrimp, peeledanddeveined
- 2 tablespoonsoliveoil
- 2 clovesgarlic, minced
- 1 teaspoondriedoregano
- Saltandpepper, totaste
- Woodenormetalskewers
- Lemonwedges (forserving)

TzatzikiSauceIngredients:

- 1 one cup of Greek yogurt
- 1/2 cucumber, grated and squeezed to remove excess moisture
- 2 clovesgarlic, minced
- 1 tablespoonfreshlemonjuice
- 1 tablespoonextravirginoliveoil
- 1 tablespoonfreshdill, chopped
- Saltandpepper, totaste

DetailedDirections:

1. Preheat the grill to medium-high heat.
2. In a bowl, combine the shrimp, olive oil, minced garlic, dried oregano, salt, and pepper. Make sure to evenly coat the shrimp with the mixture.
3. Place the shrimp on skewers, making sure to leave a small gap between each shrimp for even cooking.
4. To cook the shrimp skewers, carefully place them on the grill that has been preheated. Allow the shrimp to cook for approximately 2 to 3 minutes on each side, or until they turn a vibrant pink color and are thoroughly cooked.

5. While the shrimp is being grilled, use this time to make the delightful tzatziki sauce. Combine Greek yogurt, grated cucumber, minced garlic, lemon juice, olive oil, chopped dill, salt, and pepper in a bowl. Be sure to mix the ingredients well to create a perfectly blended and harmonious sauce.
6. Take the shrimp skewers off the grill and serve them hot, accompanied by tzatziki sauce and lemon wedges as side options.

Nutritional breakdown per serving:

Calories: 200 kcal, Protein: 24 grams, Carbohydrates: 5 grams, Fat: 10 grams, Saturated Fat: 2 grams, Cholesterol: 220 milligrams, Sodium: 300 milligrams, Fiber: 1 grams, and Sugar: 2 grams.

SHRIMP PASTA

Total Cooking Time: 20 minutes

Prep Time: 15 minutes

Servings: 4 servings

Ingredients:

- 1 pound long pasta
- 1 pound large peeled and deveined shrimp (18 to 20 count), tails on or off
- 4 tablespoonsunsaltedbutter
- 3 tablespoonsextra-virginoliveoil
- 1/2 cup thinly sliced garlic (about 7 cloves)
- Kosher salt (such as Diamond Crystal)

DetailedDirections:

1. To prepare the pasta, carefully follow the instructions provided on the package to achieve the desired al dente texture. Once cooked, drain the pasta thoroughly and set it aside for future use.
2. Introduce the thinly sliced garlic into the skillet and cook it until it becomes aromatic and obtains a light golden color, which usually takes around 2 minutes.
3. Place the sliced garlic in the skillet and cook it over medium heat for approximately 2 minutes until it becomes aromatic and obtains a gentle golden hue.
4. Place the shrimp into the skillet and allow them to cook until they achieve a vibrant pink color and are thoroughly cooked, typically taking around 3 to 4 minutes per side.
5. Season with salt to taste.
6. Combine the cooked pasta with the garlic and shrimp in the skillet, ensuring that the pasta is evenly coated.

Nutritional breakdown per serving:

Calories: 302 kcal, Protein: 20 grams, Carbohydrates: 32 grams, Fat: 8 grams, Saturated Fat: 2 grams, Cholesterol: 120 milligrams, Sodium: 250 milligrams, Fiber: 4 grams, and Sugar: 6 grams.

GREEK-STYLE GRILLED SARDINES

Total Cooking Time: 4-6 minutes
Prep Time: 5 minutes
Servings: 2-4 servings

Ingredients:

- 600 grams (1.3 pounds) wholefreshsardines
- 3 tablespoonsoliveoil
- 1 teaspoonkoshersalt
- Dried oregano (to serve with)
- Lemon quarters (to serve with)

DetailedDirections:

1. Preheat the grill to medium-high heat.
2. Prepare the sardines by rinsing them under water and removing any scales. You can leave the innards intact or cut the fish up the middle and remove them if desired.
3. In a small bowl, mix together the olive oil and kosher salt.
4. Brush both sides of the sardines with the olive oil and salt mixture.
5. Place the sardines on the preheated grill and cook over direct heat until well-charred, about 2-3 minutes per side.
6. Utilizing a metal spatula or fish turner, delicately turn the sardines over and continue grilling for an extra 2 minutes, or until the second side achieves a charred appearance and the sardines are fully cooked.
7. Transfer the grilled sardines to a large platter and season with salt.
8. Garnish with dried oregano and serve with lemon quarters for squeezing over the sardines.

Nutritional breakdown per serving:

Calories: 251 kcal, Protein: 29 grams, Carbohydrates: 16 grams, Fat: 10 grams, Saturated Fat: 2 grams, Cholesterol: 16 milligrams, Sodium: 237 milligrams, Fiber: 5 grams, and Sugar: 4 grams.

SEAFOOD SKEWERS

Total Cooking Time: 15 minutes
Prep Time: 10 minutes
Servings: 4 servings

Ingredients:

- 1 pound large shrimp, peeled and deveined
- 1 poundseascallops
- 1 lb of firm white fish fillets into chunks
- 1/4 cupextra-virginoliveoil
- 2 tablespoonslemonjuice
- 2 clovesgarlic, minced
- 1 teaspoondriedoregano
- 1 teaspoondriedbasil
- 1/2 teaspoonsalt
- 1/4 teaspoonblackpepper
- Submerge wooden skewers in water for a duration of 30 minutes

DetailedDirections:

1. Preheat the grill to medium-high heat.
2. To create a tasty marinade, mix olive oil, lemon juice, minced garlic, dried oregano, dried basil, salt, and black pepper in a bowl. Continuously whisk the ingredients until they are thoroughly combined and evenly mixed.
3. Arrange the shrimp, scallops, and fish chunks on the soaked wooden skewers, alternating between the various types of seafood.
4. Brush the marinade over the seafood skewers, making sure to coat them evenly.
5. Position the skewers on the preheated grill and grill each side for approximately 3-4 minutes until the seafood is fully cooked and has a translucent appearance.
6. Retrieve the skewers from the grill and give them a short resting time before serving.
7. Enjoy the Mediterranean seafood skewers while they are still hot, and consider adding a touch of freshness by drizzling some freshly squeezed lemon juice over them.

Nutritional breakdown per serving:

Calories: 320 kcal, Protein: 42 grams, Carbohydrates: 4 grams, Fat: 14 grams, Saturated Fat: 2 grams, Cholesterol: 250 milligrams, Sodium: 600 milligrams, Fiber: 0 grams, and Sugar: 0 grams.

LEMON GARLIC SCALLOPS

Total Cooking Time: 10-15 minutes
Prep Time: 10 minutes
Servings: 4 servings

Ingredients:

- 1 poundscallops
- 2 tablespoonsoliveoil
- 2 tablespoonsunsaltedbutter
- 1 tablespoonmincedgarlic
- 2 tablespoonslemonjuice
- 1 teaspoonlemonzest
- 1 tablespoonDijonmustard
- 2 tablespoonsheavycream
- 1 teaspoonchoppeddill
- Saltandpepper, totaste

DetailedDirections:

1. In a medium-sized bowl, combine olive oil, minced garlic, lemon juice, lemon zest, Dijon mustard, heavy cream, chopped dill, salt, and pepper.
2. Using a paper towel, softly press the scallops to remove any excess moisture, ensuring they are thoroughly dried.
3. Apply medium-high heat to warm a mixture of olive oil and butter in a sizable skillet.
4. Apply a light seasoning of salt and pepper to the scallops, then gently place them in the skillet.
5. Cook the scallops for about 2-3 minutes on each side until they are golden brown and cooked through.
6. Take the scallops out of the skillet and keep them aside.
7. In a skillet, put the minced garlic and cook it over medium heat for approximately one minute until it becomes fragrant and emits its pleasant aroma.
8. Pour the lemon juice mixture into the skillet and thoroughly mix it to ensure proper combination.
9. Continue cooking for one more minute to ensure the scallops are heated through.

10. Return the scallops to the skillet and toss them in the lemon garlic sauce to coat.

11. Continue cooking for one more minute to ensure the scallops are heated thoroughly.

12. Present the Mediterranean lemon garlic scallops while they are still hot, and if desired, adorn them with fresh dill or parsley.

Nutritional breakdown per serving:

Calories: 122 kcal, Protein: 8 grams, Carbohydrates: 3 grams, Fat: 9 grams, Saturated Fat: 6 grams, Cholesterol: 37 milligrams, Sodium: 310 milligrams, Fiber: 0 grams, and Sugar: 0 grams.

SHRIMP AND CHICKPEA SALAD

Total Cooking Time: 15 minutes
Prep Time: 10 minutes
Servings: 4 servings

Ingredients:

- 1 poundshrimp, peeledanddeveined
- 2 tablespoonsoliveoil
- 2 clovesgarlic, minced
- 1 teaspoondriedoregano
- Saltandpepper, totaste
- 1 can chickpeas, drained and rinsed
- 1 cupcherrytomatoes, halved
- 1 cucumber, diced
- 1/4 cupredonion, thinlysliced
- 1/4 cup of pitted and halved Kalamata olives
- 1/4 cupcrumbledfetacheese
- Juiceof 1 lemon
- 2 tablespoonsextravirginoliveoil
- Fresh parsley, chopped (for garnish)

DetailedDirections:

1. Take a bowl and mix the shrimp with olive oil, minced garlic, dried oregano, salt, and pepper until they are well combined.
2. Before you start cooking, preheat a skillet over medium-high heat and carefully add the shrimp to the hot skillet. Cook each side of the shrimp for approximately 2-3 minutes, or until they turn pink and are fully cooked. Once done, remove from the heat source.
3. To create a delicious salad, combine the chickpeas, cherry tomatoes, cucumber, red onion, Kalamata olives, and crumbled feta cheese in a generously-sized salad bowl. Ensure that all the ingredients are mixed well for optimal flavor.
4. Transfer the cooked shrimp to the salad bowl.

5. In a small bowl, blend the lemon juice and extra virgin olive oil together by whisking them. Once the salad is prepared, evenly drizzle the dressing over the ingredients and gently toss everything together to achieve a thorough combination.
6. Garnish with fresh chopped parsley.
7. Serve the Mediterranean shrimp and chickpea salad immediately.

Nutritional breakdown per serving:

Calories: 350 kcal, Protein: 26 grams, Carbohydrates: 25 grams, Fat: 18 grams, Saturated Fat: 4 grams, Cholesterol: 180 milligrams, Sodium: 600 milligrams, Fiber: 7 grams, and Sugar: 4 grams.

LEMON HERB GRILLED FISH

Total Cooking Time: 10-12 minutes
Prep Time: 5 minutes
Servings: 4 servings

Ingredients:

- 4 fish fillets (e.g. salmon, trout, or white fish)
- 2 tablespoonsoliveoil
- Juiceof 1 lemon
- 2 clovesgarlic, minced
- 1 teaspoon dried herbs
- Salt and pepper, to taste
- Lemonwedges (forserving)

DetailedDirections:

1. Preheat the grill to medium-high heat.
2. In a small bowl, mix the olive oil, lemon juice, minced garlic, dried herbs, salt, and pepper until they are fully incorporated. Ensure all the ingredients are well blended together.
3. Apply the marinade mixture to both sides of the fish fillets using a brush.
4. Place the fish fillets onto the grill that has been preheated, and cook them for around 4-6 minutes on each side. Make sure the fish is cooked through and can be easily flaked with a fork. Keep in mind that the cooking time may vary depending on the thickness of the fillets.
5. Remove the fish from the grill and let it sit for a few minutes before serving.
6. Serve the grilled fish seasoned with lemon and herbs while it is still hot. Optionally, provide lemon wedges on the side for those who wish to squeeze fresh lemon juice over the fish.

Nutritional breakdown per serving:

Calories: 109 kcal, Protein: 23 grams, Carbohydrates: 0 grams, Fat: 1 grams, Saturated Fat: 0 grams, Cholesterol: 75 milligrams, Sodium: 347 milligrams, Fiber: 0 grams, and Sugar: 1 grams.

GRILLED MEDITERRANEAN TUNA STEAKS RECIPE

Total Cooking Time: 10 minutes
Prep Time: 5 minutes
Servings: 4 servings

Ingredients:

- 4 tuna steaks (about 6 ounces each)
- 2 tablespoonsoliveoil
- 2 clovesgarlic, minced
- Juiceof 1 lemon
- Saltandpepper, totaste
- Optional: dried oregano, red pepper flakes

DetailedDirections:

1. Preheat the grill to medium-high heat.
2. In a small bowl, mix together the olive oil, minced garlic, lemon juice, salt, and pepper using a whisk. If you prefer, you can also add a touch of dried oregano and red pepper flakes to enhance the flavor.
3. Using the marinade mixture, coat both sides of the tuna steaks with a brush.
4. Put the tuna steaks onto the grill that has been preheated and cook them for approximately 2-3 minutes per side. Ensure that the steaks are seared on the outside while still remaining pink in the center. Avoid overcooking to keep the tuna tender and juicy.
5. Take the tuna steaks off the grill and allow them to rest for a few minutes before serving.
6. Present the Mediterranean-style grilled tuna steaks while they are still hot, and add a drizzle of freshly squeezed lemon juice over them.

Nutritional breakdown per serving:

Calories: 240 kcal, Protein: 35 grams, Carbohydrates: 1 grams, Fat: 10 grams, Saturated Fat: 2 grams, Cholesterol: 75 milligrams, Sodium: 100 milligrams, Fiber: 0 grams, and Sugar: 0 grams.

MEDITERRANEAN SARDINE SALAD

Total Cooking Time: 15 minutes
Prep Time: 10 minutes
Servings: 4 servings

Ingredients:

- 2 (4-ounce) cans of sardines packed in olive oil, drained
- 2 tbsp diced red onion or shallot
- 1 tsp of lemon zest and 3 tbsp of lemon juice
- Salt, totaste
- 1 tablespoonDijonmustard
- 1 largecelerystalk, finelychopped
- Blackpepper, totaste
- Mixed salad greens, for serving (optional)

DetailedDirections:

1. In a medium-sized bowl, flake the drained sardines into small pieces.
2. Add the finely chopped red onion or shallot, grated lemon zest, lemon juice, salt, Dijon mustard, and finely chopped celery to the bowl. Mixwelltocombine.
3. Season with black pepper to taste.
4. Serve the Mediterranean sardine salad on its own or over a bed of mixed salad greens, if desired.

Nutritional breakdown per serving:

Calories: 150 kcal, Protein: 13 grams, Carbohydrates: 3 grams, Fat: 10 grams, Saturated Fat: 2 grams, Cholesterol: 30 milligrams, Sodium: 300 milligrams, Fiber: 1 grams, and Sugar: 1 grams.

MUSSELS IN WHITE WINE

Total Cooking Time: 15 minutes
Prep Time: 10 minutes
Servings: 4 servings

Ingredients:

- 2 pounds fresh mussels, cleaned and debearded
- 2 tablespoonsoliveoil
- 2 shallots, finelychopped
- 4 clovesgarlic, minced
- 1 cupdrywhitewine
- 1/4 cupchoppedfreshparsley
- Saltandpepper, totaste
- Lemonwedges, forserving
- Crustybread, forserving

DetailedDirections:

1. Slowly and attentively heat the olive oil in a sizable pot or Dutch oven over a medium heat setting until it is fully warmed.
2. Incorporate the shallots and garlic into the pot, then sauté them for approximately 2 to 3 minutes until they become soft and emit a pleasant aroma.
3. Pour the white wine into the pot and heat it gradually until it reaches a gentle simmer.
4. Place the cleaned mussels into the pot and ensure they are covered with a lid. Cook for about 5-7 minutes, shaking the pot occasionally, until the mussels have opened.
5. Remove and discard any mussels that have remained closed and have not opened during the cooking process.
6. Integrate the finely chopped parsley into the mixture and season it with salt and pepper to suit your taste, adapting based on your individual preferences.
7. Present the Mediterranean mussels in white wine while hot, accompanied by lemon wedges and crusty bread on the side for savoring with the delectable broth.

Nutritional breakdown per serving:

Calories: 250 kcal, Protein: 15 grams, Carbohydrates: 10 grams, Fat: 8 grams, Saturated Fat: 1 grams, Cholesterol: 30 milligrams, Sodium: 400 milligrams, Fiber: 1 grams, and Sugar: 15 grams.

SHRIMP AND AVOCADO SALAD RECIPE

Total Cooking Time: 15 minutes
Prep Time: 10 minutes
Servings: 4 servings

Ingredients:

- 1 pound large shrimp, peeled and deveined
- 2 tablespoonsoliveoil
- 1 teaspoondriedoregano
- Saltandpepper, totaste
- 4 cupsmixedsaladgreens
- 1 cupcherrytomatoes, halved
- 1 cucumber, diced
- 1 redbellpepper, diced
- 1/4 cupredonion, thinlysliced
- 1 avocado, diced
- 1/4 cup of pitted and halved Kalamata olives
- 1/4 cupcrumbledfetacheese
- Juiceof 1 lemon
- 2 tablespoonsextravirginoliveoil
- Fresh parsley, chopped (for garnish)

DetailedDirections:

1. Transfer the shrimp to a bowl and thoroughly combine them with olive oil, dried oregano, salt, and pepper, ensuring that each shrimp is evenly coated with the mixture.
2. Place the skillet on medium-high heat and carefully add the shrimp to it. Cook for around 2 to 3 minutes on each side until the shrimp turn pink and are cooked thoroughly. Afterward, remove the skillet from the heat source.
3. Take a large salad bowl and mix together the salad greens, cherry tomatoes, cucumber, red bell pepper, red onion, avocado, Kalamata olives, and crumbled feta cheese.
4. Place the cooked shrimp into the salad bowl.

5. In a small bowl, whisk together the lemon juice and extra virgin olive oil. Evenly distribute the dressing over the salad and carefully toss to incorporate all the ingredients.
6. Garnish with fresh chopped parsley.
7. Serve the Mediterranean shrimp and avocado salad immediately.

Nutritional breakdown per serving:

Calories: 320 kcal, Protein: 24 grams, Carbohydrates: 14 grams, Fat: 20 grams, Saturated Fat: 4 grams, Cholesterol: 220 milligrams, Sodium: 480 milligrams, Fiber: 6 grams, and Sugar: 4 grams.

SHRIMP SCAMPI

Total Cooking Time: 15 minutes
Prep Time: 10 minutes
Servings: 4 servings

Ingredients:

- 1 poundshrimp, peeledanddeveined
- 4 tablespoonsbutter
- 4 clovesgarlic, minced
- 1/4 cupdrywhitewine
- Juiceof 1 lemon
- 1/4 cupchoppedfreshparsley
- Saltandpepper, totaste
- Crushed red pepper flakes (optional)

DetailedDirections:

1. Place the butter in a large skillet and heat it over medium heat until it completely melts.
2. Incorporate the minced garlic into the skillet and sauté it for approximately 1 minute, or until it becomes aromatic.
3. Add the shrimp to the skillet and cook them for about 2 to 3 minutes on each side until they turn pink and become opaque in texture.
4. Take the shrimp out of the skillet and set them aside, keeping them reserved for future use.
5. In the same skillet, pour in the white wine and lemon juice. Let the mixture reach a low simmer and cook for 2-3 minutes until it undergoes a slight reduction.
6. Return the shrimp to the skillet and toss them in the sauce to coat.
7. Incorporate the chopped parsley into the mixture and season it with salt, pepper, and crushed red pepper flakes according to your preference.
8. Continue cooking for one more minute to ensure the shrimp is thoroughly heated.
9. Serve the Mediterranean shrimp scampi hot, garnished with additional parsley if desired.

Nutritional breakdown per serving:

Calories: 250 kcal, Protein: 25 grams, Carbohydrates: 4 grams, Fat: 14 grams, Saturated Fat: 8 grams, Cholesterol: 250 milligrams, Sodium: 400 milligrams, Fiber: 0 grams, and Sugar: 0 grams.

TUNA BRUSCHETTA

Total Cooking Time: 20 minutes
Prep Time: 15 minutes
Servings: 8 servings

Ingredients:

- 1 pound of plum tomatoes, which is approximately 4 to 5 large tomatoes, or substitute with another ripe tomato variety
- 1 teaspoonkoshersalt
- 5 tablespoonsextra-virginoliveoil
- 2 largegarliccloves, minced
- 8 largebasilleaves
- Grilled or toasted crusty bread, for serving
- 1 (2.6 oz.) pouch of chunk light tuna in water
- 1/4 cupfinelyshreddedParmesancheese

DetailedDirections:

1. Cut the tomatoes into small cubes and move them to a colander. Sprinkle salt over the tomatoes and allow them to sit for a period of time to let the excess moisture drain out.
2. In a bowl, combine the drained tomatoes, minced garlic, extra-virgin olive oil, and torn basil leaves. Mixwelltocombine.
3. Toast or grill the crusty bread slices until they are golden brown and crispy.
4. Spread the tomato mixture generously over each slice of bread.
5. Top each bruschetta with a portion of the chunk light tuna and sprinkle with shredded Parmesan cheese.
6. Serve the Mediterranean tuna bruschetta as an appetizer or light meal.

Nutritional breakdown per serving:

Calories: 203 kcal, Protein: 3 grams, Carbohydrates: 16 grams, Fat: 15 grams, Saturated Fat: 2 grams, Cholesterol: 0 milligrams, Sodium: 263 milligrams, Fiber: 3 grams, and Sugar: 5 grams.

GRILLED CALAMARI

Total Cooking Time: 10 minutes
Prep Time: 5 minutes
Servings: 4 servings

Ingredients:

- 1 to 1 1/2 pounds of whole, cleaned calamari. If frozen, ensure that it is thawed before use
- 5 tablespoonsoliveoil
- 2 clovesgarlic, minced
- 1 teaspoondriedoregano
- 2 tablespoons of fresh lemon juice in the dish and keep a few lemon wedges aside for serving
- 1/2 teaspoonsalt
- 1/4 teaspoonfreshlygroundblackpepper

DetailedDirections:

1. Preheat the grill to medium-high heat.
2. Create a marinade by blending together olive oil, minced garlic, dried oregano, lemon juice, salt, and black pepper in a bowl.
3. Slice the calamari bodies crosswise into 1/2-inch rings.
4. Place the calamari rings in the marinade and toss to coat them evenly.
5. Thread the calamari rings onto skewers or place them directly on the grill grates.
6. Grill the calamari for 2-3 minutes per side until they are opaque and lightly charred.
7. Remove the calamari from the grill and serve hot, garnished with lemon wedges.

Nutritional breakdown per serving:

Calories: 137 kcal, Protein: 25 grams, Carbohydrates: 1.7 grams, Fat: 2 grams, Saturated Fat: 1 grams, Cholesterol: 162 milligrams, Sodium: 469 milligrams, Fiber: 0 grams, and Sugar: 1 grams.

LEMON GARLIC BUTTER GRILLED SHRIMP

Total Cooking Time: 10 minutes
Prep Time: 5 minutes
Servings: 4 servings

Ingredients:

- 1 pound large shrimp, peeled and deveined
- 2 tablespoonsoliveoil
- 4 clovesgarlic, minced
- 2 tablespoonsfreshlemonjuice
- 1 teaspoonlemonzest
- Saltandpepper, totaste
- Fresh parsley, chopped (for garnish)

DetailedDirections:

8. Preheat the grill to medium-high heat.
9. In a mixing bowl, combine the olive oil, minced garlic, lemon juice, lemon zest, salt, and pepper. Stir the ingredients together until they are thoroughly blended and evenly incorporated.
10. Place the shrimp in the bowl and gently mix them with the marinade, ensuring that they are evenly coated.
11. Place the shrimp on skewers, making sure to leave a small gap between each shrimp for even cooking.
12. Place the shrimp skewers onto the grill that has been preheated and cook for around 2 to 3 minutes on each side, or until the shrimp turn pink and are cooked through.
13. Take the shrimp skewers off the grill and move them to a plate for serving.
14. Garnish with freshly chopped parsley.
15. Present the grilled shrimp with lemon garlic butter while hot, and offer extra lemon wedges on the side for those who prefer to squeeze additional lemon juice over the shrimp.

Nutritional breakdown per serving:

Calories: 180 kcal, Protein: 23 grams, Carbohydrates: 2 grams, Fat: 9 grams, Saturated Fat: 1 grams, Cholesterol: 220 milligrams, Sodium: 260 milligrams, Fiber: 0 grams, and Sugar: 0 grams.

LEMON DILL BAKED SALMON

Total Cooking Time: 25 minutes
Prep Time: 10 minutes
Servings: 4 servings

Ingredients:

- 4 salmonfillets (6 ounceseach)
- 2 tablespoonsoliveoil
- 1 1/2 teaspoonslemonzest
- 2 tablespoonsfreshlemonjuice
- Salt and freshly ground black pepper
- 1 tablespoonchoppedfreshdill

DetailedDirections:

1. To prepare for baking, set the oven temperature to 400°F (200°C) in advance by adjusting the temperature controls.
2. Put the salmon fillets into a baking dish that has been lightly greased.
3. In a bowl, thoroughly blend the olive oil, lemon zest, and lemon juice by whisking them together until well combined.
4. Drizzle the mixture over the salmon fillets, ensuring they are well coated.
5. Tailor the seasoning of the salmon by incorporating salt and freshly ground black pepper to meet your preferred taste.
6. Evenly distribute the freshly chopped dill on the surface of the salmon.
7. Cook the salmon in the preheated oven for about 12 to 15 minutes, or until it is thoroughly cooked and can be effortlessly flaked with a fork.
8. Remove the salmon from the oven and let it sit for a short while before serving.
9. Serve the lemon dill baked salmon hot, garnished with additional fresh dill if desired.

Nutritional breakdown per serving:

Calories: 320 kcal, Protein: 26 grams, Carbohydrates: 2 grams, Fat: 22 grams, Saturated Fat: 9 grams, Cholesterol: 104 milligrams, Sodium: 197 milligrams, Fiber: 4 grams, and Sugar: 6 grams.

CHAPTER 5
FISH AND SEAFOOD

HONEY AND YOGURT PARFAIT

Total Cooking Time: 15 minutes
Prep Time: 10 minutes
Servings: 1 parfait.

Ingredients:

- 1 cup Greek yogurt (vanilla or plain)
- Fruit of choice (such as strawberries, blueberries, or mixed berries)
- Honey
- Toppings of choice (such as granola, nuts, or cinnamon)

DetailedDirections:

1. Cut up your choice of fruit into bite-sized pieces.
2. Arrange the fruit in layers at the bottom of a glass or mason jar.
3. Place a layer of Greek yogurt on top of the fruit.
4. Repeat the layers of fruit and yogurt until the glass or jar is filled.
5. Gently drizzle honey over the uppermost layer of yogurt, providing a touch of sweetness to complement the tanginess of the Greek yogurt.
6. Add any desired toppings, such as granola, nuts, or a sprinkle of cinnamon.
7. Store the parfait in the refrigerator until ready to eat.
8. If using granola, nuts, or cereals as toppings, add them right before eating to maintain their crunchiness.

Nutritional breakdown per serving:

Calories: 270 kcal, Protein: 13 grams, Carbohydrates: 36 grams, Fat: 9 grams, Saturated Fat: 2 grams, Cholesterol: 10 milligrams, Sodium: 200 milligrams, Fiber: 4 grams, and Sugar: 35 grams.

CITRUS SORBET

Total Cooking Time: 10 minutes
Prep Time: 10 minutes
Servings: 1 serving

Ingredients:

- Zestof 1 lemon
- Zestof 1 tangerine
- 1 cupwater
- 1 cupsugar
- Freshmintleaves (optional)
- Juiceof 1 lemon
- Juiceof 1 tangerine
- Juiceof 1 orange

DetailedDirections:

1. Remove the zest from 1 lemon and 1 tangerine using a vegetable peeler, reserving the fruit.
2. In a medium saucepan, combine the lemon and tangerine zest, water, sugar, and mint leaves (if using).
3. Simmer the mixture, stirring occasionally, until it reaches a gentle boil. Keep the mixture cooking for an additional 1 to 2 minutes, making sure that the sugar is fully dissolved and the flavors have seamlessly combined into a delightful harmony.
4. Take the saucepan off the heat source and allow the mixture to cool down.
5. After it has cooled down, strain the syrup to separate the zest and mint leaves.
6. Squeeze the juice from the lemon, tangerine, and orange into a separate container.
7. Combine the citrus juice with the cooled syrup and mix well.
8. Pour the mixture into an ice cream maker and adhere to the manufacturer's instructions to churn it until it achieves a smooth texture resembling that of sorbet.
9. Move the sorbet to a container with a lid and place it in the freezer for a few hours to allow it to solidify.
10. Serve the citrus sorbet in bowls or cones and enjoy!

Nutritional breakdown per serving:

Calories: 220 kcal, Protein: 2 grams, Carbohydrates: 54 grams, Fat: 0 grams, Saturated Fat: 0 grams, Cholesterol: 0 milligrams, Sodium: 0 milligrams, Fiber: 3 grams, and Sugar: 1 grams.

FRESH FIG BRUSCHETTA

Total Cooking Time: 15 minutes
Prep Time: 5 minutes
Servings: 1 parfait.

Ingredients:

- Freshfigs, ripe (4-6 figs)
- Baguetteorcrustybreadslices
- Oliveoil
- Balsamicglazeorreduction
- Optional toppings: goat cheese, honey, arugula, prosciutto, etc.

Detailed Directions:

1. Before you begin, adjust the oven temperature to the specific heat setting indicated in the recipe.
2. Slice the baguette or crusty bread into thin slices.
3. Using a brush, apply olive oil to both sides of the bread slices.
4. Gently position the bread slices on a baking sheet and transfer them to the preheated oven, taking care to arrange them in a tidy manner. Let the slices toast until they develop an attractive golden brown color and a delightful crispy texture.
5. While the bread is toasting, wash and slice the fresh figs into thin slices.
6. After toasting the bread slices, take them out of the oven and allow them to cool down for a short while.
7. Arrange the fig slices on top of each bread slice.
8. Optional: Add toppings such as goat cheese, honey, arugula, or prosciutto to enhance the flavors.
9. Drizzle balsamic glaze or reduction over the fig-topped bread slices.
10. Serve the fresh fig bruschetta immediately and enjoy!

Nutritional breakdown per serving:

Calories: 200 kcal, Protein: 10 grams, Carbohydrates: 30 grams, Fat: 6 grams, Saturated Fat: 1 grams, Cholesterol: 0 milligrams, Sodium: 0 milligrams, Fiber: 5 grams, and Sugar: 10 grams.

GREEK YOGURT WITH GRILLED STONE FRUITS AND MINT

Total Cooking Time: 15 minutes

Prep Time: 10 minutes

Servings: 4 servings

Ingredients:

- 4 cupsofGreekyogurt
- 4 peaches or nectarines, halved and pitted
- 1 tablespoonofhoney
- Freshmintleaves, forgarnish

DetailedDirections:

1. Preheat your grill to medium-high heat.
2. Using a brush, apply honey to the cut sides of the peaches or nectarines.
3. Place the peaches or nectarines, cut side down, on the grill.
4. Grill for about 5-7 minutes, or until the fruit is slightly charred and softened.
5. Take the grilled fruit off the grill and allow it to cool for a few minutes.
6. In serving bowls or glasses, spoon about 1 cup of Greek yogurt.
7. Top each serving with a grilled peach or nectarine half.
8. Garnish with fresh mint leaves.

Nutritional breakdown per serving:

Calories: 110 kcal, Protein: 10 grams, Carbohydrates: 5 grams, Fat: 6 grams, Saturated Fat: 3 grams, Cholesterol: 15 milligrams, Sodium: 40 milligrams, Fiber: 0 grams, and Sugar: 5 grams.

GRILLED PEACHES WITH GREEK YOGURT AND HONEY

Total Cooking Time: 15 minutes
Prep Time: 5 minutes
Servings: 4 servings

Ingredients:

- 4 medium ripe peaches, cut in half
- 1/2 cup honey flavored fat-free Greek yogurt
- 4 tablespoonsofhoney
- Cinnamon (totaste)

DetailedDirections:

1. Place the peaches cut side down on the grill.
2. Place the peaches on the grill over low or indirect heat and cook until they become soft, which usually takes around 2 to 4 minutes per side.
3. Combine the yogurt and cinnamon.
4. Place 1 tablespoon of yogurt over each peach half.
5. Drizzlewithhoney.

Nutritional breakdown per serving:

Calories: 132 kcal, Protein: 12 grams, Carbohydrates: 22 grams, Fat: 5 grams, Saturated Fat: 1 grams, Cholesterol: 5 milligrams, Sodium: 185 milligrams, Fiber: 4 grams, and Sugar: 12 grams.

WATERMELON AND FETA SALAD WITH MINT

Total Cooking Time: 15 minutes
Prep Time: 5 minutes
Servings: 4 servings

Ingredients:

- 1/4 cupextra-virginoliveoil
- 2 tablespoonsredwinevinegar
- 0.5 teaspoonofkoshersalt
- 3 cups of seedless watermelon, cut into cubes
- 1 cup of cucumber, medium-sized and chopped
- 1 cupcrumbledfeta
- 1 cup of crumbled feta cheese
- 1/2 cup of mint, coarsely chopped, and reserve some for garnishing
- Flaky sea salt, for garnish (optional)

DetailedDirections:

1. In a small bowl, blend the olive oil, red wine vinegar, and kosher salt until they are fully integrated, ensuring they are well combined.
2. In a spacious bowl, mix the watermelon cubes, cucumber chunks, crumbled feta cheese, sliced red onion, and chopped mint leaves together until well blended.
3. Pour the dressing evenly over the watermelon mixture and delicately toss it to ensure everything is well combined.
4. Garnish with additional mint leaves and flaky sea salt, if desired.
5. Serveimmediatelyandenjoy!

Nutritional breakdown per serving:

Calories: 269 kcal, Protein: 7 grams, Carbohydrates: 12 grams, Fat: 0 grams, Saturated Fat: 1 grams, Cholesterol: 33 milligrams, Sodium: 525 milligrams, Fiber: 2 grams, and Sugar: 10 grams.

GREEK YOGURT WITH HONEY AND PISTACHIOS

Total Cooking Time: 5 minutes
Prep Time: 5 minutes
Servings: 1 serving

Ingredients:

- 1 cupofGreekyogurt
- 1 tablespoonofhoney
- 2 tablespoonsofpistachios, chopped

Directions:

1. Put the Greek yogurt into a bowl.
2. Drizzle the honey over the yogurt.
3. Sprinkle the chopped pistachios on top.
4. Thoroughly blend the ingredients together until well combined.
5. Serveandenjoy!

Nutritional breakdown per serving:

Calories: 300 kcal, Protein: 12 grams, Carbohydrates: 22 grams, Fat: 8 grams, Saturated Fat: 4 grams, Cholesterol: 6 milligrams, Sodium: 127 milligrams, Fiber: 5 grams, and Sugar: 8 grams.

DELICIOUS GREEK YOGURT PARFAIT WITH FRESH BERRIES AND SWEET HONEY

Total Cooking Time: 5 minutes
Prep Time: 5 minutes
Servings: 1 serving

Ingredients:

- 1 cup Greek yogurt (plain or flavored)
- 1/2 cup of assorted fresh berries such as strawberries, blueberries, or raspberries
- 2 tablespoonshoney
- Optional: granola or nuts for topping

Directions:

1. In a glass or a bowl, layer half of the Greek yogurt.
2. Place half of the fresh berries on the yogurt as a topping.
3. Pour one tablespoon of honey over the berries, allowing it to drizzle evenly.
4. Continue layering the remaining Greek yogurt, berries, and honey in the same manner as before.
5. Top with granola or nuts, if desired.
6. Serveimmediatelyandenjoy!

Nutritional breakdown per serving:

Calories: 300 kcal, Protein: 24 grams, Carbohydrates: 28 grams, Fat: 5 grams, Saturated Fat: 0 grams, Cholesterol: 10 milligrams, Sodium: 100 milligrams, Fiber: 2 grams, and Sugar: 15 grams.

GREEK YOGURT WITH GRILLED NECTARINES AND HONEY

Total Cooking Time: 10 minutes
Prep Time: 5 minutes
Servings: 1 servings

Ingredients:

- 1 ripenectarine
- 1/2 cupGreekyogurt
- 1 tablespoonhoney

Directions:

1. To prepare for use, heat the grill or grill pan over medium heat.
2. Cut the nectarine in half and remove the pit.
3. Place the nectarine halves on the grill, cut-side down.
4. Cook on the grill for approximately 2-3 minutes, until grill marks are visible and the nectarines have slightly softened.
5. Remove the nectarines from the grill and let them cool for a minute.
6. In a serving bowl, spoon the Greek yogurt.
7. Place the grilled nectarine halves on top of the yogurt.
8. Drizzle the honey over the nectarines and yogurt.

Nutritional breakdown per serving:

Calories: 300 kcal, Protein: 10 grams, Carbohydrates: 26 grams, Fat: 5 grams, Saturated Fat: 0 grams, Cholesterol: 0 milligrams, Sodium: 100 milligrams, Fiber: 5 grams, and Sugar: 10 grams.

CHOCOLATE DIPPED STRAWBERRIES

Total Cooking Time: 15 minutes
Prep Time: 10 minutes
Servings: 20 strawberries

Ingredients:

- 24 fresh strawberries, rinsed and pat dried
- 2 cupsmilkchocolatechips
- 2 tablespoonscoconutoil

Directions:

1. Cover a spacious baking sheet with parchment paper.
2. Mix together the milk chocolate chips and coconut oil in a microwave-safe bowl until they are well combined.
3. Microwave the chocolate mixture in 30-second intervals, pausing to stir in between, until it is fully melted and becomes smooth in texture.
4. Hold a strawberry by its stem and immerse it into the melted chocolate, gently swirling it to ensure all sides are coated.
5. Remove the strawberry from the chocolate, letting any extra chocolate drip off.
6. Place the chocolate-dipped strawberry on the prepared baking sheet.
7. Continue the dipping process with the remaining strawberries, ensuring they are spaced apart to prevent them from touching.
8. Refrigerate the strawberries for 15 minutes to set the chocolate.
9. Remove the strawberries from the refrigerator and let them harden completely at room temperature.
10. Serve the chocolate-dipped strawberries the same day, if possible.

Nutritional breakdown per serving

(1 chocolate-dipped strawberry): Calories: 80 kcal, Protein: 1 grams, Carbohydrates: 9 grams, Fat: 5 grams, Saturated Fat: 3 grams, Cholesterol: 0 milligrams, Sodium: 2 milligrams, Fiber: 1 grams, and Sugar: 8 grams.

GREEK YOGURT MOUSSE WITH FRESH FRUIT

Total Cooking Time: 10 minutes
Prep Time: 10 minutes
Servings: 4 servings

Ingredients:

- 2 cupsGreekyogurt
- 2 tablespoonshoney
- 1 teaspoonvanillaextract
- 1 cup of assorted fresh fruits, such as berries, sliced peaches, or chopped mango
- Fresh mint leaves, for garnish (optional)

Directions:

1. Mix the Greek yogurt, honey, and vanilla extract together in a mixing bowl. Stir until the mixture is smooth and well blended.
2. Divide the Greek yogurt mixture into serving glasses or bowls.
3. Top each serving with a generous amount of mixed fresh fruits.
4. Garnish with fresh mint leaves, if desired.
5. Serve the Greek yogurt mousse with fresh fruit immediately.

Nutritional breakdown per serving:

Calories (1 serving): 150 kcal, Protein: 15 grams, Carbohydrates: 22 grams, Fat: 0 grams, Saturated Fat: 0 grams, Cholesterol: 10 milligrams, Sodium: 50 milligrams, Fiber: 1 grams, and Sugar: 19 grams.

LEMON LAVENDER MADELEINES

Total Cooking Time: 15 minutes
Prep Time: 10 minutes
Servings: 12 madeleines

Ingredients:

- 2/3 cupall-purposeflour
- 1/2 teaspoonbakingpowder
- 1/4 teaspoonsalt
- 2 largeeggs
- 1/2 cupgranulatedsugar
- 1 tablespoonlemonzest
- 1 teaspoondriedlavenderbuds
- 1/2 teaspoonvanillaextract
- 1/2 cup of melted unsalted butter that has been cooled
- Powdered sugar, for dusting (optional)

Directions:

1. To get started, double-check that the oven has been preheated to a temperature of 375°F (190°C). Then, prepare a madeleine pan by greasing it and lightly dusting it with flour to ensure the madeleines do not stick.
2. Combine the all-purpose flour, baking powder, and salt in a small bowl, whisking them together until they are thoroughly combined. Once mixed, set the mixture aside for future use.
3. Using a spacious mixing bowl, whisk together the eggs and granulated sugar until they become light in color and have a fluffy texture.
4. Add the lemon zest, dried lavender buds, and vanilla extract to the egg mixture. Mixwell.
5. With caution, incorporate the flour mixture into the egg mixture by gently folding it in, ensuring thorough combination without overmixing.
6. Gradually drizzle the melted butter into the batter, stirring gently until it is completely blended.

7. Using a spoon, fill each mold of the prepared madeleine pan with batter, filling them approximately 3/4 full.
8. Transfer the batter to the preheated oven and let it bake for around 10 minutes, or until the madeleines acquire a golden brown hue on the edges and regain their shape when gently pressed.
9. Remove the madeleines from the oven and let them cool in the pan for a few minutes
10. Carefully transfer the madeleines to a wire rack to cool completely.
11. Dust the cooled madeleines with powdered sugar, if desired.
12. Serve the lemon lavender madeleines with a cup of tea or coffee.

Nutritional breakdown per serving:

Calories (1 madeleine): 80 kcal, Protein: 1 grams, Carbohydrates: 8 grams, Fat: 3 grams, Saturated Fat: 0 grams, Cholesterol: 30 milligrams, Sodium: 30 milligrams, Fiber: 0 grams, and   Sugar: 5   grams.

CHOCOLATE DIPPED STRAWBERRIES

Total Cooking Time: 15 minutes
Prep Time: 5 minutes
Servings: 20 strawberries

Ingredients:

- 24 freshstrawberries, rinsedanddried
- 2 cupsmilkchocolatechips
- 2 tablespoonsshortening

Directions:

1. Place a large baking sheet and cover it with parchment paper.
2. In a bowl that is safe for use in the microwave, mix together the milk chocolate chips and shortening.
3. Warm up the chocolate mixture in the microwave, making sure to pause and stir every 30 seconds, until it has completely melted and achieved a smooth texture.
4. Hold a strawberry by its stem and submerge it into the melted chocolate, gently swirling it to ensure all sides are coated.
5. Let any extra chocolate drip off, then carefully transfer the chocolate-coated strawberry onto the baking sheet that has been prepared in advance.
6. Continue dipping the remaining strawberries, ensuring that they are spaced apart to avoid touching.
7. Refrigerate the strawberries for 15 minutes to set the chocolate.
8. Once chilled, take the strawberries out of the refrigerator and allow them to fully solidify at room temperature.
9. Serve the chocolate-dipped strawberries the same day, if possible, for the best taste and texture.

Nutritional breakdown per serving:

Calories (1 strawberry): 80 kcal, Protein: 1 grams, Carbohydrates: 9 grams, Fat: 5 grams, Saturated Fat: 3 grams, Cholesterol: 0 milligrams, Sodium: 2 milligrams, Fiber: 1 grams, and Sugar: 8 grams.

GREEK YOGURT WITH GRILLED WATERMELON AND MINT

Total Cooking Time: 15 minutes
Prep Time: 10 minutes
Servings: 4 servings

Ingredients:

- 4 thickslicesofwatermelon
- 1 tablespoonoliveoil
- 2 cupsGreekyogurt
- 2 tablespoonshoney
- Freshmintleaves, forgarnish

Directions:

1. Before you start cooking, ensure that the grill or grill pan is heated to medium-high temperature.
2. Using a brush, apply a layer of olive oil to both sides of the watermelon slices.
3. Put the watermelon slices onto the grill and cook for approximately 2-3 minutes on each side, or until grill marks become visible.
4. Remove the grilled watermelon slices from the grill and let them cool slightly.
5. Cut the grilled watermelon into bite-sized cubes.
6. In serving bowls or glasses, layer the Greek yogurt and grilled watermelon cubes.
7. Drizzle the honey over the top.
8. Garnish with fresh mint leaves.
9. Serve the Greek yogurt with grilled watermelon and mint immediately and enjoy!

Nutritional breakdown per serving:

Calories: 180 kcal, Protein: 10 grams, Carbohydrates: 24 grams, Fat: 6 grams, Saturated Fat: 2 grams, Cholesterol: 10 milligrams, Sodium: 50 milligrams, Fiber: 1 grams, and Sugar: 20 grams.

GREEK YOGURT WITH FRESH BERRIES AND PISTACHIO CRUMBLE

Total Cooking Time: 15 minutes
Prep Time: 10 minutes
Servings: 2 servings

Ingredients:

- 1 cupGreekyogurt
- 1/2 cup mixed fresh berries (blueberries, strawberries, raspberries)
- 2 tablespoonscrushedpistachios
- 1 tablespoonhoney

Directions:

1. In serving bowls or glasses, divide the Greek yogurt evenly.
2. Top the Greek yogurt with fresh berries.
3. Sprinkle the crushed pistachios over the berries.
4. Drizzle honey over the top.
5. Serve the Greek yogurt with fresh berries and pistachio crumble immediately and enjoy!

Nutritional breakdown per serving:

Calories: 200 kcal, Protein: 12 grams, Carbohydrates: 23 grams, Fat: 8 grams, Saturated Fat: 1 grams, Cholesterol: 10 milligrams, Sodium: 50 milligrams, Fiber: 3 grams, and Sugar: 17 grams.

CHOCOLATE CINNAMON TOAST

Total Cooking Time: 10 minutes
Prep Time: 5 minutes
Servings: 1 serving

Ingredients:

- 1 slice of bread (such as white, whole wheat, or brioche)
- 1 tablespoonunsaltedbutter
- 1 tablespoongranulatedorbrownsugar
- 1/2 teaspoongroundcinnamon
- 1 tablespoon chocolate chips or grated chocolate

Directions:

1. In a small bowl, mix together the sugar and ground cinnamon.
2. Toast the bread until golden brown.
3. Once the bread is warm, evenly spread the unsalted butter over one side of the toast, ensuring full coverage.
4. Ensure that the cinnamon sugar mixture is evenly spread over the buttered side of the toast, making certain that it is thoroughly coated.
5. Sprinkle the chocolate chips or grated chocolate over the cinnamon sugar layer.
6. Put the toast under the broiler for approximately one minute, or until the chocolate begins to melt.
7. Remove the toast from the broiler and let it cool slightly before serving.

Nutritional breakdown per serving (1 slice):

Calories: 174 kcal, Protein: 2 grams, Carbohydrates: 33 grams, Fat: 5 grams, Saturated Fat: 1 grams, Cholesterol: 0 milligrams, Sodium: 284 milligrams, Fiber: 2 grams, and Sugar: 14 grams.

ORANGE SALAD

Total Cooking Time: 15 minutes
Prep Time: 10 minutes
Servings: 4 servings

Ingredients:

- 4 largeoranges
- 1/4 cuppomegranatearils (seeds)
- Fresh mint leaves, for garnish (optional)

Directions:

1. Peel the oranges and slice them into rounds or segments.
2. Arrange the orange slices neatly on a serving platter or on individual plates.
3. Sprinkle the pomegranate arils over the oranges.
4. Garnish with fresh mint leaves, if desired.
5. Serve the Mediterranean orange salad immediately and enjoy!

Nutritional breakdown per serving:

Calories: 80 kcal, Protein: 1 grams, Carbohydrates: 20 grams, Fat: 0 grams, Saturated Fat: 0 grams, Cholesterol: 0 milligrams, Sodium: 0 milligrams, Fiber: 4 grams, and Sugar: 16 grams.

DATE BALLS

Total Cooking Time: 15 minutes
Prep Time: 10 minutes
Servings: 12 servings

Ingredients:

- 1 cuppitteddates
- 1/2 cupalmonds
- 1/2 cupwalnuts
- 1/4 cupunsweetenedshreddedcoconut
- 1 tablespoonhoney
- 1 teaspoonlemonzest
- 1/2 teaspoongroundcinnamon
- Pinchofseasalt

Directions:

1. In a food processor, combine the pitted dates, almonds, walnuts, shredded coconut, honey, lemon zest, ground cinnamon, and sea salt.
2. Pulse the mixture until it comes together and forms a sticky dough.
3. Take approximately one tablespoon of the mixture and use your palms to roll it into a ball shape.
4. Repeat the process with the remaining mixture to make more date balls.
5. Place the date balls on a plate or baking sheet lined with parchment paper.
6. Refrigerate the date balls for at least 30 minutes to firm up.
7. Serve the Mediterranean date balls chilled and enjoy!

Nutritional breakdown per serving (1 date ball):

Calories: 90 kcal, Protein: 2 grams, Carbohydrates: 0 grams, Fat: 5 grams, Saturated Fat: 1 grams, Cholesterol: 0 milligrams, Sodium: 0 milligrams, Fiber: 2 grams, and Sugar: 8 grams.

FIG AND RICOTTA CROSTINI

Total Cooking Time: 15 minutes
Prep Time: 10 minutes
Servings: 12 servings

Ingredients:

- 1 French baguette, cut into 1/2 inch slices
- 1 (15 ounce) containerricottacheese
- 12 fresh basil leaves, cut into thin strips
- 8 black mission figs, cut into quarters
- 1/4 cupagedbalsamicvinegar

Directions:

1. To preheat the oven, set the temperature to 375 degrees Fahrenheit (190 degrees Celsius).
2. Position the baguette slices on a baking sheet lined with foil, ensuring that no grease is applied.
3. Put the bread into the oven that has been preheated and bake it until the bottoms become brown, which usually takes around 5 minutes.
4. After flipping the bread, allow it to bake for another 5 minutes until it becomes crisp. Once done, remove the pan from the oven.
5. Evenly distribute 1 tablespoon of ricotta onto every slice of toasted bread.
6. Place a basil leaf on top of the ricotta on each slice.
7. Arrange a quarter of a fig on top of the basil on each slice.
8. Gently pour the aged balsamic vinegar over the figs, ensuring even coverage.
9. Serve the fig and ricotta crostini immediately and enjoy!

Nutritional breakdown per serving

(1 crostini): Calories: 110 kcal, Protein: 4 grams, Carbohydrates: 17 grams, Fat: 3 grams, Saturated Fat: 2 grams, Cholesterol: 10 milligrams, Sodium: 100 milligrams, Fiber: 1 grams, and Sugar: 4 grams.

CITRUS SALAD

Total Cooking Time: 15 minutes
Prep Time: 5 minutes
Servings: 4 servings

Ingredients:

- 4 naveloranges
- 4 bloodoranges
- 2 small ruby or Oro Blanco grapefruits
- 2 small fennel bulbs, thinly sliced into rings after trimming
- 2 large shallots or small red onion, thinly sliced into rings
- 1/2 cup pitted olives, such as Moroccan oil-cured black or Castelvetrano green olives
- Fresh mint leaves, for garnish (optional)

Directions:

1. To start, cut off the ends of the orange and grapefruit. Stand them vertically on a cutting board and cautiously employ a sharp knife to peel away the skin and white pith, carefully following the fruit's natural contour.
2. Hold each peeled fruit over a large bowl to catch the juice. Slice the fruit crosswise into rounds, about 1/4-inch thick, and remove any seeds.
3. Add the sliced fennel, shallots or red onion, and olives to the bowl with the citrus slices.
4. Gently mix the salad to incorporate all the ingredients.
5. Move the salad onto a serving platter or onto individual plates.
6. If desired, decorate with fresh mint leaves as a garnish.
7. Serve the Mediterranean citrus salad immediately and enjoy!

Nutritional breakdown per serving (1/4 of the recipe):

Calories: 120 kcal, Protein: 2 grams, Carbohydrates: 27 grams, Fat: 2 grams, Saturated Fat: 0 grams, Cholesterol: 0 milligrams, Sodium: 150 milligrams, Fiber: 6 grams, and Sugar: 18 grams.

CONCLUSION

In conclusion, the "15 Minutes Mediterranean Meals" cookbook is an exceptional culinary resource that revolutionizes the way we approach cooking and eating. With its emphasis on quick and effortless meal preparation, this cookbook provides a gateway to the vibrant and healthful world of Mediterranean cuisine.

By providing an array of recipes that encompass a wide variety of flavors and can be prepared in a mere 15 minutes, this cookbook effectively meets the needs of individuals with busy, contemporary lifestyles, all while ensuring that taste and nutritional value remain uncompromised. From delectable appetizers and refreshing salads to satiating main courses and indulgent desserts, the cookbook covers a wide spectrum of Mediterranean flavors that will entice and satisfy the taste buds.

Beyond the convenience factor, the "15 Minutes Mediterranean Meals" cookbook is a treasure trove of culinary wisdom and inspiration. It educates readers about the fundamental principles of the Mediterranean diet, highlighting the use of fresh, locally sourced ingredients, whole grains, lean proteins, and healthy fats. By adopting this dietary approach, individuals can unlock a multitude of health advantages, such as a decreased likelihood of heart disease, enhanced cognitive function, and an extended lifespan.

Moreover, this cookbook goes beyond just providing recipes. It encourages readers to adopt a holistic approach to their well-being by promoting mindful eating and fostering a connection to the food we consume. It emphasizes the importance of savoring each bite, engaging in communal dining experiences, and celebrating the rich cultural heritage associated with Mediterranean cuisine.

The "15 Minutes Mediterranean Meals" cookbook is an invaluable tool for individuals of all cooking skill levels. Its accessible and easy-to-follow recipes, accompanied by beautiful visuals, empower even the most novice cooks to create delicious and wholesome meals with confidence and creativity. The cookbook also offers practical tips for efficient meal planning, time-saving techniques, and ingredient substitutions, making it adaptable to individual preferences and dietary requirements.

In a world where time is of the essence, the "15 Minutes Mediterranean Meals" cookbook stands out as a beacon of hope, demonstrating that healthy and flavorful meals can be prepared quickly and enjoyed by everyone. It bridges the gap between convenience and nourishment, inspiring individuals to prioritize their well-being without compromising on taste or quality.

In summary, the "15 Minutes Mediterranean Meals" cookbook goes beyond being a mere compilation of recipes. It serves as a transformative guide, empowering individuals to fully embrace the Mediterranean way of life and cultivating a balanced and harmonious connection between food, health, and happiness.By integrating the core principles and delightful flavors of the Mediterranean diet into our everyday routines, we have the opportunity to embark on a gastronomic adventure that not only improves our physical health but also nurtures our inner being. So, grab your apron, unleash your creativity, and embark on a flavorful adventure with the "15 Minutes Mediterranean Meals" cookbook as your trusted companion.